No More Rejections

Rejections

50 SECRETS TO WRITING A MANUSCRIPT THAT SELLS

ALICE ORR

No More Rejections. Copyright © 2004 by Alice Orr. Manufactured in the United States of America. All rights reserved. No part of this book may be reproduced in any form or by any electronic or mechanical means including information storage and retrieval systems without permission in writing from the publisher, except by a reviewer, who may quote brief passages in a review. Published by Writer's Digest Books, an imprint of F + W Publications, Inc., 4700 East Galbraith Road, Cincinnati, Ohio 45236. (800) 289-0963. First edition.

Visit our Web site at www.writersdigest.com for information on more resources for writers.

To receive a free weekly e-mail newsletter delivering tips and updates about writing and about Writer's Digest products, register directly at our Web site at http://newsletters.fwpublications.com.

08 07 06 05 04   5 4 3 2 1

Library of Congress Cataloging-in-Publication Data

Orr, A. (Alice)
    No more rejections : 50 secrets to writing a manuscript that sells / by Alice
Orr.—1st ed.
        p. cm.
    Includes index.
    ISBN 1-58297-285-0 (alk. paper)
        1. Authorship—Marketing. 2. Authorship. I. Title.

PN161.O77 2004
070.5′2—dc22   2003064598
                                                                       CIP

Edited by Michelle Ruberg
Designed by Davis Stanard
Production coordinated by Robin Richie

DEDICATION

To Jonathan and Maya June—the Lights of my Life

ABOUT THE AUTHOR

Alice Orr has a wide range of experience in writing and publishing—as book editor, literary agent, published author, teacher, and lecturer. Alice teaches and lectures nationally with two lecture series currently available for bookings. The first of these series is titled *No More Rejections: An Insider's Guide to Regaining Power Over the Fate of Your Manuscript.* Alice's second lecture series is titled *How to Stop Shooting Your Writing Career in the Foot: An Insider's Guide to Regaining Power Over Your Fate in the Publishing Business.* You may contact Alice by e-mail at AorrTalk@aol.com for further information.

Alice has two grown children and two perfect grandchildren and shares residence between New York City and Vashon Island, Washington.

ACKNOWLEDGMENTS

At just about the time I was finishing the first draft of this book, a former client of mine, Karen Plunkett Powell, passed away. Karen was more than a client to me; she was also an editor, and on occasion, a collaborator. Back in the late 80's, she encouraged me to write a book about the publishing business—my take on the territory from the multiple perspectives of author, editor, and literary agent. I was already lecturing on the subject in a series titled "How to Stop Shooting Your Writing Career In the Foot." Karen and I agreed to co-write a book by the same name. I taped my lectures, and she transcribed them. She was a whiz at the Macintosh, so she was able to earmark everything for ready accessibility, even the one-liners that I spun off the top of my head on the dais then immediately forgot, until Karen retrieved them. As it turned out, I was too immersed in my multiple careers to pursue that project for long. We shelved it and said, "Maybe later." Later never happened.

Writing this book brought that old one to mind, and I thought about calling Karen to consider resurrecting the project. She'd been ill but had assured me, and everyone else she knew, that she would definitely pull through. We believed her; at least I did. Karen was a fighter. Unfortunately, she lost that battle, and I lost a significant member of the extended family of my life. I would have asked her to edit this book, but she was gone too soon. I hope it is up to her standards. If I ever write the book she and I planned all those years ago, there will be a memory of Karen on every page, just like there is a memory of her forever in my heart.

In a lighter vein, thought with equal sincerity, I wish to acknowledge so many who have helped and inspired me along the way. I thank, first of all, the greatest teachers of writing, writers themselves, so many and various throughout my life as a bookophile. Specifically, and most recently, I thank the women of the first writing critique group I have ever been privileged to attend—Jill Andres, Rachel Bard, Kaj Wyn Berry, and Ann Spiers. They have jerked my toes off the wrong track more than once. I thank also the dedicated professionals—book editors and literary agents—who have been my mentors and role models throughout my career. Special gratitude belongs, in spades, to my own literary agent, Denise Marcil. She is the best of the best, no question about it. Thanks to my editors on this project as well, Donya Dickerson and Rachel Vater who helped me develop the book and Michelle Ruberg who nurtured it through to the end.

As I state in this book, I identify with place, and that includes the places I find to squirrel myself away in a corner and write. In this regard, I thank the proprietors of Café Luna, Vashon Island, Washington for allowing me to tap away at my laptop, plugged into their electricity, taking up a table in their establishment for hours on end till this book was finally finished. Thanks also to my cousin, Shelley Bance, for offering Upper Westside digs as yet another squirreling corner. Most of all, I thank my husband and partner in life, Jonathan Orr, for the warm place he has made for me in his heart. I thank him for hours upon hours of reading and listening to my work and for having the courage it takes to tell a writer-spouse what needs to be changed about that work and why.

For all of this and all of you, I am grateful and blessed, both in large measure.

TABLE OF CONTENTS

INTRODUCTION

BIRD ON THE SHOULDER

Every writer I know has endured rejection. If any among you have escaped this fate, maybe you should be writing this book instead of me—because I'm a writer and my work has been rejected many times. There may be an element of masochism in the writerly character. Otherwise, how do we explain our willing, even clamorous, participation in work where rejection is the norm and acceptance is the exception?

My own road to no has been a broad one. On the occasion of my first major rejection, the editor implied—or maybe she said straight out—that I had no idea what I was doing. My big mistake in that situation, aside from writing the book in the first place— titled, as I recall, *A Tender Quest*—was agreeing to a sushi lunch. I didn't know sushi from tsunami. I'd heard it had something to do with eating raw fish, a notion that still fails to attract me. On the other hand, this was my editor making the suggestion. I wanted to appear cooperative, so I replied, "What can it hurt? I'll give sushi a try." Had I understood the purpose of this particular luncheon, I'd have given a different response.

I didn't have a clue, though I probably should have. This was my second novel for this editor. The first had been published five months after we went to contract on the second. We were by now a few months past that first publication, and so far my debut as a novelist hadn't set the world afire. If I'd known even the basics of the business, I'd have understood what this lackluster performance boded for my career in commercial publishing. As I said, I didn't have a clue.

Even so, there were other omens I should have picked up on. My second novel had quested its way, and not all that tenderly, through an original submission plus two extensive revisions. I was at the point where I'd pretty much lost track of what the story was originally about. As I took a wobbly chopstick grip on my third portion of raw something or other wrapped in seaweed, my editor let me know she felt the same.

"This just doesn't work for us," she said.

I think she may also have apologized, but that nicety failed to register. My mind was elsewhere. Her pronouncement had plunged me into shock, but I was suddenly no longer clueless. I was stone-cold certain. There would be no more revision chances. *A Tender Quest* had gone down the plumbing, taking months of my work along with it. Sushi slipped from its precarious perch between my chopsticks and plummeted to the edge of my plate.

"You seem to think a little bird sat on your shoulder and told you the secret of how to write that first book," my editor was saying. "Like you didn't have anything to do with it."

I couldn't respond. I excused myself and dashed to that upscale restaurant's upscale ladies room. I leaned my clammy forehead against the cool tiles of the black marble stall and struggled to keep my insides under control. Meanwhile, I tried to figure out what she'd meant. Bird on my shoulder? What was she talking about? I'd never been aware of anybody, feathered creature or otherwise, sharing writing secrets with me. What I had always been aware of was my helplessness. I felt like a child. Because of the way the writing world works, I had no control over my work's destiny. I wanted this power back, desperately. Suddenly, I understood how perilous cluelessness can be.

If you've ever submitted a manuscript, you know what I'm talking about. You labor over your work. You send it out into what feels like a void. Then, you wait for a thumbs up or down on your efforts, your ambitions, your hope. You endure this because you have no idea what else you can do. You are as clueless as I was in that ladies room with my forehead pressed against tile as black as I believed my future to be.

A couple of years after the scene in the sushi restaurant, I became an in-house book editor. This career choice had a lot to do with power. I was still determined to regain mine. I was also determined to share its secrets. Eventually, I discovered I could do that most effectively as a literary agent. I could be that bird my first editor told me about. I could sit on my client's shoulder and whisper in her ear the words she needed to hear to avoid demoralizing rejection scenarios of her own. I could do that because something very basic had changed since my black-marble ladies room days. My years on the other side of the desk had taught me a lot about creating publishable fiction.

I'd studied and read and taught. I'd worked with authors of commercial fiction—also referred to as popular fiction—at varying levels of ability. I've done years more of that since, including countless critiques of novels, proposals for novels, and synopses of novels. Some of my most passionate writing is scribbled in manuscript margins. I saved many of those annotated pages for precisely that reason, because they reveal my best thoughts on the writing craft and how to improve the practice of that craft.

Those critiques (with details altered to protect the authors' identities) inform the pages of this book. They represent the real-life writing of many real-life authors, some published, some not. In the first passage regarding idea formation, which is internal and therefore difficult to critique for anyone other than oneself, I explore weaknesses in my own work. Occasionally, I also employ examples from storytelling classics. To all of that, I add my professional experience—as long-time teacher and lecturer on the subjects of writing and publishing, as book editor for a New York City publisher, as president of my own Manhattan-based literary agency.

Few experiences are more upsetting to an author than rejection of his work. We open the envelope, and there it is: "This just doesn't work for us." For a writer, not much could feel worse. I wish I had a talisman to share with you against such times—a guarantee they'd never happen again—but I don't. What I do offer are my years of experience and expertise, and to be a bird on your shoulder with empowering secrets to whisper in your ear.

Passage 1

THE IDEA FROM HEAVEN. . . . OR ELSEWHERE

The writing-as-journey metaphor has been done to death. Nonetheless, it works, so here goes yet again. I hear you crying "Uncle," insert my earplugs, and continue.

The shortest distance between departure point and destination is, as we've all known since seventh grade, a straight line. Every wrong turn delays arrival. Take enough of these detours and you lose your way entirely. The authors of the manuscript examples I critique in this book strayed from their original course toward a publishable manuscript. They disregarded the rules of that road and ended up weakening their stories and undermining the impression those stories made.

I've selected the specific storytelling wrong turns I examine in this book because they are common ones. I've blundered into them myself on occasion. In fact, in this first passage in particular, I use my own recent work as a prime example of the kind of stumbling and misdirection that can lead an author far afield from where he wants to be—on the acceptance pile of his editor or agent of choice.

Fortunately, for every wrong turn there's at least one way back on track again. In the ten passages that make up this book, I focus on my secrets to redirecting your work when you've gone astray. That is where taking back your power comes in. You have the power to steer your novel clear of storytelling misjudgments. If you make one of those missteps anyway, you have the power to stop, re-think, and correct course. To access that power, you need two things. Number one—a heads-up alert to the signs that warn of a wrong turn ahead. Number two—a clear and direct guide back to the main road for the times you miss the warning signs. The pages that follow offer both.

The guidance I offer is, by the way, specifically directed toward authors of commercial fiction or, if you prefer, popular fiction. This is the publishing niche where I have spent most of my career, as editor, literary agent, and author. What I say here may or may not apply to other categories of writing. I leave that for you to judge.

Secret #1: The Wrong Idea About Ideas

In my experience, the major misconception about story ideas has to do with what an idea can and cannot accomplish. Let me illustrate with a cocktail party scenario that goes something like this:

Author stands at edge of crowd to maximize observation potential. Since this is Savvy Author, his glass contains sparkling water, diet cola or plain tonic with lime—keeping the head clear in case anyone even remotely connected with publishing should appear and require sober impressing. Fellow partier sidles over but is, unfortunately, anything but a publishing professional. Partier discovers that Author is, in fact, an author and suggests some variation of the following:

"I've got a terrific idea for a novel. Best-seller for sure. How's about I tell you my idea, you write the story, and we split the take fifty-fifty?"

More than one misconception is in play here. First of all, this non-writer underestimates the writing process. Famous sportswriter Red Smith once famously said, "There's nothing to writing. All you do is sit down at the typewriter and open a vein." The party guy with the great story idea knows nothing of this bloodletting aspect of the writer's journey. Worse yet, he doesn't understand that an idea is not a story.

An idea is only a kernel. That kernel may possess the potential to grow into the next Danielle King Mary Higgins Grisham opus— or it may not. Either way, tons of nurture, strain, frustration, doubt, and even bloodletting must be applied between planting and harvest. A clever idea may be a jumping-off place, but without the sweat equity required, the storyteller is in for a hard fall.

Not only non-writers are susceptible here. I've experienced the exhilaration of what I can only describe as a technicolor idea striking. A story concept, maybe just a scene, appears unexpectedly. Lightning in the mind reveals something entirely new, previously unimagined. "This is it," I cry out in creative ecstasy, preferably where no one is listening. "This is the story I have to write."

The problem is that I don't really have a story. I only have an idea, and an idea is only a beginning. A story, particularly in the commercial arena, requires a plot with a beginning, middle, and end. At best, my flash of inspiration will get me through the opening scene, maybe the first chapter. Without a lot more work, the story tumbles downhill from there. Too many fledgling authors ignore this danger and submit work that is, basically, a boffo beginning followed by premature denouement.

Any editor worth her blue pencil will see straight through the technicolor bit to its lackluster follow-up. Even if she's impressed by the story start, she'll know there's no second act. Once upon a time, in the days of Henry Higgins cum Maxwell Perkins, she might have taken this author on anyway, made him a mission, a protégé. Guess where those days have gone and how long they'll be there? Let's go back to my flash of idea and do some rethinking. Maybe this brainstorm has provided me with a situation upon which I could build a story. To be foundation material, an idea must have two components.

1. Compelling characters. An idea flash may reveal a set of intriguing, even startling circumstances. Unless those circumstances happen to equally intriguing characters, an editor will soon cease to care. Intriguing characters come to life on the page. Each has a history fraught with complex experiences, a personality riddled with contradictions. Anything less provides poor fodder for storytelling. Such characters are layered and complicated, often confused, and they are in conflict with each other.

2. Conflict potential. The conflict inherent in the idea must have the power to reach beyond the initial story situation. That conflict must have the power to propel the editor/reader, nonstop and without much respite, from first scene to last with a riveting transit between. A powerful story idea plants that conflict kernel deep. A powerful storyteller cultivates that kernel through obstacles, frustrations, near misses, and reversals as layered and complex as the characters themselves. Conjuring all of that requires opening the vein Red Smith spoke of.

Secret #2: Keep the Idea Muscle In Shape

Would you feel better or worse if I told you I still get rejections? Recently, that's exactly what happened.

I published several romantic suspense novels, took some time off to be a grandma, then decided to try bigger books with more suspense and less romance. One night, I had a dream so vivid I woke up trembling, short of breath and convinced that the goddess of scenarios had sent me a best-seller for sure. What I'd actually experienced was one of those technicolor idea strikes I mentioned. A lightning bolt pierced my sleep and left me with an idea that wasn't a story. Too bad I didn't recognize this. Have you ever fallen in love? Do you recall how your good judgment took a hike for the duration? I'd fallen in love with that riveting scene from my predawn dream. I couldn't see or reason anything else, and I couldn't wait to write it down.

I took myself back into the scary dark place of that nightmare, straight down to the bowels of it, and wrote what I felt and saw. I honed that scene until the impact was razor-sharp. The trouble was I didn't have a story to go with it. I figured my boffo first scene would carry through the rest. Thus deluded, I completed the fifty pages of text my agent had asked to see. Good thing she wasn't expecting a synopsis, because I didn't really have a story.

Are you surprised my agent was less than impressed? She didn't even mention my non-synopsis. I had been right about one thing. She loved the opening. After that, her response rapidly lost steam. The pacing wasn't strong enough. She felt no urgency. As for the all-important protagonist's voice, beyond the opening scene, she didn't really have one. I'd built expectations with my opener, then squandered them.

The ice-water bath of her critique had shocked me out of my post-idea-strike euphoria at last. My next submission would have to be on the mark and then some to make up for this faux pas. Thank heaven I was back in my right mind again, because I had some regrouping to do, all the way back to the essential question: "What am I going to write about?" Filmmaker David Lynch, author and director of some of the most imaginative screen scenarios ever, says, "Ideas dictate everything. You have to be true to that or you're dead."

Yet, there always is pressure to write what will sell. I was piling that pressure on myself when I conceived my ill-fated proposal with the boffo opening and no follow-through. I was writing what I thought would turn my agent on, instead of seeking the conflicted heart of my story and writing from that place. I call the idea that makes the heart of a story beat the idea from heaven. I could have started with my dream inspiration and coaxed depth and richness from it. I could have made it into my idea from heaven. I forgot I possessed the power to accomplish that. What, specifically, should I have remembered to do?

Imagine for a moment that the imagination is a muscle. To condition the imaginative muscle, to make that muscle equal to the rigors of the storytelling task, we give it a daily workout. If I'd gone from terrifying dream to imagination exercise mat, instead of straight into writing, the results would have been very different. Here is the five-step exercise I should have done.

1. Pick the time of day most fertile for your imagination. For me, that's immediately after waking, close to the state that produced my terrifying dream. Pen and pad are ready ahead of time. I believe imagination and writing voice are best accessed in longhand. I urge you not to do this exercise on a computer. (I used to think night was my most imaginative time but found that being tired encouraged me to natter on for pages I'd later have to excise. Midday, frenzied with activity and interruptions, is almost nobody's best imaginative time.)

2. Decide which method of recording ideas works best for you. You can use a notebook, cards, even a tape recorder. Taping works for many verbal people. Try different possibilities before deciding which does the trick for you.

3. Pose yourself a question. "Where does the story go from here?" Or, "What does my protagonist do next?" Take time fashioning your most pressing question, but don't obsess over it. Trust your writerly instinct to know what your story needs. (This exercise can be performed at any point in the writing process, addressing the story stage you're at "right now" and what to do next. Always use a current writing project as subject ground for any writing exercise. That way, no effort is wasted on the random or general. If you don't have a current writing project to work on, get one.)

4. Begin coming up with answers to the question you've posed. Never settle for the first answer that comes. Keep thinking and responding. Push yourself to make the answers to your question more original, less expected, as you burrow deeper into the situation and its characters. Encourage your mind to run wild.

5. Record each idea as it comes. Record for no longer than ten to fifteen minutes. Don't censor your responses in any way. Don't say, "That's too outlandish," or "This won't work." Record everything, without critiquing or evaluating. At the end of the ten or fifteen minutes, put down your pen or turn off the tape recorder.

After you've finished recording ideas, sit for a moment and take note of how you feel. This may be a sixth step, because it is as important as the rest. I predict you'll feel stimulated, full of mental energy, ready to spin off still more ideas in a cannonade of creativity. Your imaginative muscle has had a workout. Do this every day.

You'll find yourself being more creative than ever before, and enjoying it, too.

I robbed myself of that enjoyment when I neglected to take time for this exercise as preparation for developing my story idea and writing my story proposal. My flabby imagination muscle failed me because I failed it. Learn from my negative example. Take power over your own creative laziness, and give your story idea the strength it needs to succeed.

Secret #3: Get Into Trouble

The exercise you've just learned takes you into the most intuitive, least controlled levels of your consciousness. The next phase of your search for the idea from heaven happens somewhere almost opposite to that. The next phase weeds through the ideas you've generated to pinpoint those that work best for your story.

What exactly makes an idea a troublemaker? You've completed the five-step exercise and taken a break to cool down a bit. It's time to ask yourself, "Which ideas, among all these I've generated, have the most complication inherent in them?" Specifically, which promise the most complication between characters? Which ideas put my characters in passionate opposition to one another? These are the ideas with the greatest capacity to lend conflict and interest to your story. The more passionate, the better.

Next, ask yourself, "Could this complication lead to trouble, especially for my protagonist?" Writer/director/producer Mike Nichols says this about storytelling: "All we care about is the humanity." Characters are the true focus of our fascination with stories—characters in trouble and conflict and how they react in extreme circumstances to resolve their predicament, or fail to resolve it. Trouble and conflict make us care enough about a story to keep turning pages. Trouble and conflict always have something to do with one or more of the following dramatic themes.

Betrayal	Guilt	Duty	Cowardice
Deceit	Loss	Heroism	Devotion
Obsession	Greed	Redemption	Hatred
Envy	Privation	Disgrace	Love
Revenge	Sacrifice	Cruelty	Compassion

Look at the list you've generated from the five-step exercise. If you've tape-recorded your ideas, transcribe them onto paper or cards for accessibility. Examine the list for evidence of these dramatic themes. Mark ideas that have the most potential for creating trouble and conflict. Do this quickly, without pondering. Find your own most compelling story material and separate it from the rest.

If you haven't been using note cards, I suggest you begin doing so. Write each of your most potent ideas on a separate card. Later, you will make additional notes on each card for each of these ideas. Here's how:

1. Think of each potent idea in terms of how it evokes one of the dramatic themes listed above. Think of your character in the dramatically charged situation this theme or state of consciousness creates. Ask, "How does my character feel in this situation? What does she do? What happens to her?"

2. Keep responses concrete. Focus on the outside of the character, her behavior. You are concerned with the character's emotional journey as she goes through this experience. But what does she *do* in

response to those emotions and while she's feeling them? How do we *see* those emotions manifest in her behavior? When you write the scene evolving from this story idea, how will the character illustrate what she's feeling via specific, concrete actions?

Again, perform this note taking phase rapidly, without stopping to contemplate. Let your instinct and imagination take charge, and do so as energetically as you can manage. When you've finished, you can arrange the cards chronologically, as they will appear in your story line, or in order of story potency—whatever feels most useful for you. What matters at this stage is that you've produced your own dramatic story material. You've piled up heaps of trouble for your characters, and you've done so out of your own fertile, thoroughly exercised imagination.

Story ideas and situations that immerse characters in trouble are pay dirt for a fiction writer. These situations are often uncomfortable to read. They carry the reader into that trouble along with the character. So why are they popular with readers? Because the consequences they create for characters, the actions and reactions they force from those characters, are intense—dramatic, exciting, compelling, and highly charged.

Intensity is a basic essential of strong storytelling, especially for today's readers and editors. Contemporary authors write for an audience conditioned by visuals. Most of the stories we experience come to us via movies and television. The imperative of the filmmaker is to hold audience attention. This is even more crucial for television, where the writer and producer have channel-surfers to contend with. Cinematic stories must grab the audience and refuse to let go until the credits roll. They must be intense.

Which doesn't mean they have to be slam-bam action mayhem

and car chases. But they do have to engage the viewer emotionally. This engagement occurs as effectively with a strong family drama as with a shoot 'em up thriller as long as, in both cases, the story keeps moving. Small, relatively uneventful, gently paced stories simply don't make it at the box office, or the ratings box, anymore. If you can name an exception to that, the rarity of that exception proves the rule.

Which brings us back to storytelling without benefit of visuals. We write for an audience conditioned in its storytelling expectations by movies and television. The author who wants to sell his commercial fiction to an editor disregards this reality at his own peril. There are, of course, readers who enjoy a slow, deep read, but they're in the minority, and they tend to prefer literary over popular fiction. The mandate of the editor in the latter venue is to acquire books that will sell in considerable numbers, not to a minority. In my ill-fated proposal, I disregarded these realities and put my future as a novelist in peril.

What exactly did I do?

As established, I started with a shocking occurrence in the prologue, graphically portrayed. This scene was also a shocker to write. I went deep into my character, forcing myself to experience, second by second, what she experienced. The effect was terrifying. I heated up the trouble she was in to an all but unbearable degree. When I finished, I breathed a sigh of relief and said, "Thank heaven that's over."

After that experience, I needed to write something less wrenching for a while. I should have scribbled some postcards or answered my e-mail. I shouldn't have gone straight on to the first chapter, but I did. As I read that chapter now, I can feel how fatigued I was with intensity, how tired I was of trouble. I recognize myself escaping into narrative.

The prologue was about event, what happened, how my protagonist reacted, no time to ponder. In chapter one, I retreated from that scary surface of intense action directly into my character's thoughts about what happened in the years since the prologue. I kept that up for pages and pages, using long paragraphs of description. The temperature of the story chilled. I'd removed my protagonist from trouble and put my story in trouble instead. My idea from heaven headed somewhere unheavenly.

Secret #4: Don't Let the Enemies Get You Down

I'm writing this on Epiphany morning. That's the twelfth day of Christmas, which means it's time to take down the tree, dismantle the centerpieces, switch back to the usual dinnerware, pack up the dozens of geegaws of the season that fill the house and return to the regular round of the rest of the year. Nobody tells me to make such a production of the holidays. Everybody seems to enjoy it, but they don't insist I do it. The priority is mine, and now the priority to strike the set is mine also.

But I have this book to write! Pressure, stress, expectations. First phalanx of the army of enemies of the idea from heaven. I tell you to open up to the inspiration of life on one hand and the depth of your imagination on the other, to let go and drift among whatever images, thoughts or fragments may be out there or in there. Yet, it's tough to let go when you feel yourself inundated by demands, wherever they may originate.

It would be handy for a writer to have someone who fields the demands of the world, catches them up and organizes them away before they reach the study door. Since helpmates are unavailable to just about all writers, a responsible person finds it difficult to

ignore the lurking expectations of others. I'm not necessarily advo-
cating self-centeredness, though some self-consideration wouldn't
hurt. I do advocate asking these questions of every task that comes
your way: "Does this really have to be done? Done by me? If so,
why? Could someone else do it? If not, why not?" Volunteers for
my holiday dismantling committee, please, raise your hands.

The demands you make on yourself require the same scrutiny.
Can you lower your standards in some non-writing areas? Do you
want your legacy to be perfectly folded laundry, a plaque naming
you employee of the decade, or a shelf of books with your name
on the spine? Life is about choices. This one you must make over
and over each day in large and small ways. Defeating the external
and internal demanders takes vigilance on behalf of your writing
and imagining time.

The puritan ethic is also right up there in the front ranks of the
enemies of creativity. Our culture too often sends the message, subtle
or not, that creative work isn't really work at all. We've been conditioned since Plymouth Rock to believe (1) Idle hands do the devil's
business, (2) If you love something passionately, you should feel
guilty about pursuing it, (3) If an activity comes naturally, even
easily, it can't be worthwhile. Such thinking is an anathema to creativity and must be defied. Suggested act of defiance: Once a day,
do nothing but stare at the wall and let the ideas come.

An accomplished poet of my acquaintance refers to another demand we authors make on ourselves as Great Masters Syndrome. I
first heard her use that term in a feminist context, since so many
of the great masters are men and that can be daunting to women
writers, but I think this one applies across the gender divide.
Whether we think of ourselves as having Shakespeare peering over
one shoulder and James Joyce or Virginia Woolf or Eudora Welty

over the other, the effect can be equally intimidating. The verdict
we pronounce upon our work in comparison to these masters is
bound to be, "Not good enough, third-rate, why even bother?" I
suggest a strong dose of get-over-it. Tell yourself to do the best you
can, and do it. Or you risk falling victim to idea block even before
writer's block has a chance to set in.

Great Masters Syndrome is just one permutation of the most
insidious of all enemies of the creative process: self-doubt. Anxiety
in general can stop the psyche cold. Insecurity and self-doubt are
chief among creativity chillers. Realistic self-criticism is a good thing.
Paralyzing self-censorship is not. I've wasted a lot of my own time
detouring into the land of not-good-enough, a head trip not worth
taking but hard to avoid. An act of will is required. The appropriate
self-admonition is, "STOP THAT RIGHT NOW!" I've said it to
myself. I say it to you. Suspend your disbelief in yourself, or the
negatives will lock you in their clutches and out of the state of free
mind and spirit where ideas reside and flow. So, let's make a battle
plan against the enemies of the idea from heaven.

Battle Strategy One: Calm down. The scattering emotions of anxiety
erect a wall of nervousness between you and your own creative
spirit. Find a technique that works for calming yourself down. Deep
breathing works for me. A few minutes of that, and I'm chilled out
altogether. Plus, I always have a pad and pen close by in case all
that heavenly calm produces an idea from on high.

Battle Strategy Two: Make the enemies your friends. When you do find
yourself in one of those negative, anxious states of mind—insecure,
fearful, angry, paranoid, resentful, vengeful, hurt—use it to your writerly advantage. If you can't get out of it, go deeper into it, see what

comes, write it down. There are stories in that darkness, ideas and thoughts you won't come up with in your sunnier moments. And, by the time you finish writing, much of the down-dragging energy of these emotions will have dissipated. You've taken power over their destructiveness and used it constructively. This advice applies equally to jet lag, hangovers, PMS, and exhaustion. When the day-to-day controls drop away, ideas come. Write them down.

Battle Strategy Three: Turn life conflict into story conflict. Another huge upheaver of the psychic smooth ground is our human tendency to get into dustups with other people. First scenario: You've had a terrible quarrel with your sister-in-law, best friend, worst enemy, or parking lot attendant. Second scenario: You've discovered something infuriating about someone. You're angry, maybe not homicidal, but definitely pissed off. That undercurrent could go on disturbing your state of mind for quite some time. Again, take advantage. Write out the details of the scene, what was said, scraps of setting detail, what each of your senses was experiencing. Above all, write your feelings, in technicolor. Exaggerate those feelings. Imagine yourself becoming homicidal. Transfer those feelings to a character in your work.

As you implement these strategies and record results, don't turn away when uncomfortable ideas come. I call these oven-cleaning ideas because, when a truly uncomfortable idea occurs to me, I'd rather clean the oven than burrow into that discomfort. Yet, therein lies pay dirt. The most powerful material in fiction, as in life, makes you cringe because it is frightening, humiliating, unsettling, distasteful, infuriating. It is intense, and you've heard my rap about that already. So don't turn away; dig in. The creepier the subject matter, the better story material it will be. Before long, you'll wade knee-deep into enemy territory and thrive all the way.

Secret #5: Avoid Idea Engine Breakdown

There still may be times your idea mechanism develops a hitch in the get-along, which can bring on an anxiety fit all its own. Once again, I exhort you to leave those jangled nerve endings at the door. The world, life, and you are jam-packed with ideas. Nevertheless, sometimes you will feel as if your tank has run dry. It hasn't. Your mind is playing games with you, running old self-doubt tapes, whispering derogatory memory voices in your ear. You must whistle an end to the games, turn off the tapes, shut down the voices. Take your pick of the following general suggestions for setting your head on a positive course. Or, move on to the Are You There Yet? section of this passage for specific exercises. All come from my trick bag of idea engine repair tools.

1. Open Up to Your Own Weirdness. David Lynch, recognized master of weirdness, says, "It's like fishing. I never know what I'm going to catch." Take yourself on an idea-fishing expedition. Don't censor or judge the strange thoughts that arise. Don't ask, "Where did *that* come from?" Disciplining this raw material, however raw it may be, comes later. For fiction, borrow the Stephen King technique of interrogating yourself. "Can I make an exciting (intense, dramatic, compelling) story out of this?" "Yes!" is the correct answer, followed by, "How?" Then, let the brainstorms rage. Take the lid off the side of yourself that embarrasses your children and makes your partner quake with dread. Let yourself go, and don't forget to take your notepad along for the ride.

2. Wake Up to the Possibilities. Speaking of notepads, you need one at your bedside. When you first wake up a good deal of your psyche is still in the alpha state, where dreams abide. Before stretching or even getting off a good yawn, grab your notepad and scribble. Write down whatever's in your head. Fragments will do. Encourage this process. Before dozing off at night, give yourself permission to wake up full of ideas in the morning. When you do, simply stay there, cozy under the covers in that still drowsy state, letting those ideas play out and be scribbled down. This can be your most imaginative time of day, and it happens *every* day.

3. Read Like A Writer. Ideas come to you when you let your mind know it's okay to let them in. This includes your reading time. I'm not talking about plagiarism. I'm talking about inspiration. You won't write the same story or the same article you're reading and claim it as your own. Instead, you will discover associations and connections that are original for you, in the parts and elements of the work you are reading. Choose a book or article in the same genre you intend to write. Or, pick something far afield. Read slowly. Allow yourself to stop and think. This is not the speed-reader route. You're reading for enrichment, mining for ideas, digging beneath the surface rather than skimming along the top, except maybe with newspaper articles, which also can be a rich resource. Never usurp the actual details of the piece. Simply reimagine them.

4. Just Write. You see the glimmer of an idea. Don't wait for the idea to perfect itself. Start writing away at it now. See where it goes. Try out possible titles. Write down a title. Come up with a first line to go with it. Make it a first line that inspires you to ask, "What will happen next?" Write a number of such lines, out of the blue, on any subject, for any situation, until one of them makes you want to know what happens next. Write on from there.

5. Build Character. Imagine two characters from the novel you're currently planning or writing. Put them in a dialogue together. Find out what they think about the situation they're in, what they think about life in general, how they're feeling at the moment. Ask them questions. What is the worst thing that ever happened to you? What do you dread most happening to you now? What was your angriest moment ever? Why were you so angry then? Are you still angry now? Explore negative experiences rather than positive ones, because negativity is the source of more conflict.

6. Be A Nosey Parker. I've become a professional eavesdropper, though I'm nowhere near as good at it as my husband, Jonathan. He has the perfect cover look, developed while riding New York City subways. His secret is to focus his eyes on the middle distance, somewhere beyond the left ear of his target victim. He's cultivated a neutral facial expression as well and, as far as I know, has never been caught in the act. Although now that I've outed him, who knows what could happen? Of course, since he's not a writer, he doesn't take notes. Taking notes demands discretion. I personally prefer ladies' rooms. I lock myself in a stall with my note cards and scribble away. I don't wait until I get home for fear I might forget a gem or two. Cafés are my favorite listening posts. I'm in one right now. Two gentlemen at the next table are roasting a third. Their chiding jocularity is 100 percent male, which I'm not. My sharp-tuned ear affords me an experience of the male psyche. Excuse me. I have to run to the ladies' room.

7. Make Lists, Lists, and More Lists. I don't know about you, but I wouldn't make it through life without lists. Those lists are usually of things to do and, maybe, how to do them. What I'm suggesting here is that you make lists of how you feel. Specifically, lists of things that make you feel intensely. What specific people, incidents, and situations evoke a strong emotional response from you? What gets you worked up? I'm not referring to issues, political or otherwise. Those tend to be more impersonal than what I'm getting at. I'm referring to people, incidents, and situations that produce a hot-blooded response. For you, they are intense. These are your personal, potent idea fodder. When you write these people as characters, these incidents or situations as scenes, you will be emotionally involved in the writing, charged up by it. That charge communicates to the reader. Storytelling pay dirt to the max.

8. Usurp the Hero. This last suggestion is more a gimmick than an exercise in originality, though creative thinking is definitely involved. Conjure any of the classic story situations with a male protagonist, a hero, at their center. Shakespeare is a fund of these, or Mark Twain, Elmore Leonard, and many others. Choose an author and that author's most dramatic story scenario, the one you find most gripping. Reinterpret that situation with a woman in the protagonist role. How would she react differently in these circumstances than her male counterpart has done? Make her a strong heroine, at least as strong as your male model. How would that strength express itself differently because she is a woman? Vive la différence.

Be careful about using that last suggestion as the basis for an actual story. This is more an exercise to get your gray cells moving than a source of actual story material, since you err dangerously close to plagiarism here. Although, with vigorous assertion of the transforming power of imagination, who knows what new and totally original twists might result? Whichever of these tactics you employ, you and your idea engine will be chugging out of the breakdown lane in no time at all.

Crossroads

AN AUTHOR SELF-INTERROGATION

Each passage in this book features a section called Crossroads, made up of questions to ask yourself related to the subject matter of that passage. Sometimes these questions will be a review of the material in the passage. Sometimes they will involve related but new material. These questions are meant to be answered in your writer's journal, a notebook or computer file that chronicles your writing experience. I combine my writer's journal with a writing work log, updated pretty much daily. This notebook incorporates my specific writing activities (a log that can be used for tax purposes to document writing as my full-time job) and a running commentary of thoughts, insights, and experiences related to my writing life (the journal). Find a form that suits you and begin your writer's journal.

IDENTIFY SUBJECT MATTER FOR YOUR FICTION

Write out the following information about yourself in detail. The more candid and complete you are in your responses, the more resource material you will have to draw from for writing ideas. Be liberal rather than conservative in your estimation of what should be included, and leave room for further additions later. For the purpose of this exercise, there is no such thing as an insignificant experience, and reticence is inappropriate. Include specific scenes or dramatized recollections wherever possible.

1. What is your ethnic background, especially your cultural experience of that ethnicity, its language, customs, foods, rituals, etc.?
2. What places have you lived long enough to know them well?
3. What have been your occupations, past and present?
4. What have been your hobbies and leisure activities, past and present?
5. What are your special abilities and areas of expertise or particular knowledge?
6. If you had to describe your physical appearance, what would you mention first?
7. How would you describe your temperament?
8. Which relationships in your life have involved conflict (in your family, in your romantic life, in your friendships, in your work life)?
9. Who have you loved intensely?
10. Who have you disliked intensely?
11. What have been your most powerful (intense, significant, formative) non-sexual experiences (during childhood, adolescence, maturity)?
12. What have been your most powerful sexual or romantic experiences?
13. What have been your personal triumphs, past and present?
14. What have been your frustrations and disappointments?
15. What are your complexes, inhibitions, and superstitions, past and present?
16. What can make you very, very angry?
17. What scares you to death?
18. What can make you unbearably sad?
19. What do you long for?
20. What do you pray won't happen to you?

21. What sort of person do you feel the most sympathy for? The least sympathy for?

22. What crime would you be most likely to commit if you were to commit a crime?

23. What act of heroism would you be least likely to perform?

24. What is the most significant thing you've ever discovered about yourself?

25. What do you like most about yourself?

26. What do you dislike most about yourself?

27. In what specific experience of your life did you feel most enraged? Terrified? Humiliated? Heartbroken? Ecstatic?

28. Feel free to add any further questions or considerations pertinent to your life and experience.

Are You There Yet?

A HANDS-ON EXERCISE

Each passage of this book features a section called Are You There Yet? This hands-on exercise is also appropriate for your writer's journal and meant to encourage your own individual practice of the principles and suggestions presented in the passage.

Here are nineteen exercises, each designed to stimulate your imagination and generate story ideas. Do them in any order that helps you kick-start your creative process.

1. Something strikes you as absurd. You wonder about it. For example, the letter labeling your subway line has been arbitrarily switched with that of another line. Make up a theory, perhaps

conspiratorial and illicit, explaining this arbitrary, even absurd occurrence. Write a scene or a story based on that theory.

2. You have a particular fear. What would happen if that fear material-
    ized? For example, what if those brakes you've been meaning to
    repair on your car gave out? Think of all the possible consequences
    of that event. Make the best of those consequences into a story
    situation or a scene for a novel.

3. Pick a particular subculture. For example, the world of horse racing
    has worked well for Dick Francis and others. Go where you can
    get closest to that environment. For example, a racetrack or off-
    track betting parlor. Watch and listen. Take notes if you can man-
    age to do so discreetly. Note, specifically, ideas for characters,
    interactions, and story situations within that setting. Write a scene
    or story.

4. Think up a catchy title, for example, "The Cat That Ran Into Walls."
    Make up a setting, characters, and story situation to go with it.

5. Think of all the personal problems a character might have. For
    example, the character is overweight. Pick the most interesting of
    those problems. Decide whether or not solving the problem is the
    object of your story. Perhaps, the problem is a permanent element
    of your characterization. Make up a story either way.

6. Think of something you are curious about. For example, what
    would it have been like to grow up in New York City in the nine-
    teenth century? Study and research the subject. Imagine the feel-
    ings and experiences of a character in that situation. Write a scene
    or a story based on that research and those imaginings.

7. When you wake up, record as much as you can remember of the
    dream you were having before waking. Make that dream into a
    waking life story, rather than a dream sequence.

8. Make a list of people who frequent a place with which you are

familiar, for example, your neighborhood Laundromat. Cast them as characters for a story or scene set in that environment.

9. Take those same people and cast them in a story or scene set in a different, maybe even extremely different, environment.

10. Pick a period of your life. For example, you might choose adolescence or college or the beginning years of your career. List the pivotal experiences of that period. Select the two most dramatic experiences from that list and build a story around them. Be sure to embellish, reimagine, and fictionalize. You're not writing memoir or autobiography.

11. Choose a favorite, or maybe a least favorite, relative. Recall an incident from that person's life, or create an incident that could have happened to that person. Build a scene or a story around that person and incident.

12. Start with a feeling—good, bad, whatever. Conjure an image you associate with that feeling. Put the image in motion with action and characters behaving in ways that suit the image and the feeling. Ask why these characters are behaving this way. What is their motivation? Develop this material into a story.

13. Think of something you own that you love. Place that object in an alien setting, somewhere it doesn't belong. Imagine that it is owned by someone other than you—someone not at all like you. Build a story around this object, its new environment, and its new owner.

14. Think of a relationship you envy—a family relationship or a romantic one or a friendship. Imagine a situation that would alienate the individuals in that relationship from one another. How might these individuals attempt to overcome that alienation? Build a story around this relationship situation.

15. Make up an interesting name or look one up in the phone book. Imagine what a character with that name might look like. Do the

same with a second name. Put these two characters together. How do they interact? Build a story around them.

16. Go out and do nothing but hunt for ideas for two hours. Make note of what you see and hear, as well as what might be going on beneath and beyond what you see and hear. Build a story around these observations.

17. Walk around the city, or your town or neighborhood. Keep going until you see something that strikes you as curious. Build a story around that curiosity.

18. Remember stories told by a previous generation of your family or acquaintance's—parents, relatives, or older friends. Choose the most interesting of those stories and build a new story around it.

19. Go through a book of photographs, or an album, of people and scenes. Choose the most interesting of those photos and build a story around it. Or, choose two photos, imagine a connection between them, and build a story around that connection.

Passage 2

WHO'S DRIVING THIS STORY?

You have a story idea strong enough to sustain your reader as a captive audience through the length of a book. Now, you must find a protagonist strong enough to do the same. Your protagonist is the center of your story around which all the rest revolves. She must carry the weight of that story from beginning to end. She must be a person of substance, complex enough to command and hold reader attention from dramatic opening page to satisfying ending.

Your protagonist must be the most fascinating person in your story, the one who makes things happen. She must never be passive, with events happening to her while she reacts rather than acts. She must be the driving principle that keeps the action of the story moving. Your protagonist is also the person with the most at stake in a story situation, and that stake creates a dilemma. Your protagonist wants a favorable resolution of this dilemma more desperately than she's ever wanted anything. The crucial intensity of this desire is a major factor in making the reader care what happens in your story, especially what happens to your protagonist.

Secret #6: Designate Your Driver Carefully

This is a heavy burden for a character to support. Can your protagonist carry the weight? Will a reader believe that, as this burden mounts with every chapter, your protagonist, though bent nearly to breaking, manages to soldier on? Or is there someone else in your story who could carry its burden more convincingly? Is your story exciting, riveting, and difficult to put down with the protagonist you have chosen—or not? The success of your story depends on how wisely you answer these questions. I propose Margaret Mitchell's *Gone with the Wind* as an example of this choice wisely made.

My first encounter with that extraordinary story was in its movie version. Since I suspect more of you have seen the movie than read the book, I refer to that film version here, specifically to the end of the first reel. Scarlett O'Hara leaves Atlanta just in time to escape Sherman's troops and returns home to the family plantation, Tara. She finds her mother dead, her father deranged, the place in a shambles, and not a scrap of food in the house. She staggers into the garden, scratches a root from the ground, attempts to eat it, and vomits. A black moment if there ever was one.

Scarlett might very well collapse onto the dusty earth, sob her heart out, and give up. The audience would certainly accept that behavior as credible, but what about the second reel? We wouldn't have one, not with Scarlett as protagonist, anyway. She'd have lost the strength to carry the story further. Instead, she makes this black moment a turning point of her story. Despite exhaustion and despair, she pushes herself up from the dirt, lifts a grimy fist to heaven, and cries, "As God is my witness, they're not going to lick me. As God is my witness, I'll never be hungry again."

Do we believe this behavior from Scarlett? She's shown herself to be selfish, shallow, uncaring, vain, indiscreet, and a passel of other things most of us don't think of as character strengths. But she's also shown herself to be stubborn, relentless, tenacious, and afire with determination. We don't doubt for an instant that she has the grit to drag herself upright and vow to God that nothing will deter her ever again. Meanwhile, we can't wait to find out how she'll go about pursuing that vow. We can't wait to see the second reel.

But, what if Scarlett O'Hara were not the protagonist of *Gone with the Wind*? What if Margaret Mitchell had chosen her other major female character, Melanie Hamilton, to be the center of the story? Melanie is certainly a better person than Scarlett, more compassionate, more virtuous, more admirable. Yet, is Melanie as capable of making things happen? She may have as much at stake as Scarlett, but how would Melanie respond to the challenge those stakes present? Would we be as eager to move on to the second reel of her story? Margaret Mitchell obviously thought not. She posed herself a difficult storytelling problem by making that choice.

One golden rule for creating a popular fiction protagonist, if you want that character to have audience appeal, is to make her heroic. In contemporary storytelling terms, I define heroism as decency. A heroic character resolves, despite formidable odds and fear of consequences, to do the right thing. She does so for admirable reasons and by generally admirable means. Readers are drawn to this protagonist because they aspire to behave as she does. It's easy to care what happens to her. Do you argue that it's not so easy to care what happens to Scarlett? Sure, she cheats, lies, and betrays. In many ways, Melanie would have been an easier sell. But Melanie would not have been capable of making as powerful an impression as Scarlett has made on generations of readers and viewers.

Scarlett O'Hara is one of the most popular characters in fiction.

Making her that notorious required brilliant storytelling. The success of Scarlett's portrayal illustrates that the drive to act decisively and dramatically, whatever the circumstances, is the first imperative in creating a compelling protagonist. Nonetheless, to the new author hoping to break in or the more seasoned writer intent upon improving status in the commercial publishing marketplace, I advise the following: Make your protagonist *both* potently active and admirably decent—in other words, Scarlett with some Melanie in her. Don't pose yourself a problem as thorny as the one Margaret Mitchell faced unless you have a character as unforgettable as Scarlett O'Hara up your sleeve. In which case, this particular golden rule is suspended, and I suspect you'll never be hungry again.

Secret #7: The Less-Is-Too-Little Hero

Changing your protagonist can give your story a new lease on life. I've critiqued many manuscripts where that was necessary. Most often, however, the flawed main characters that limp across my desk require modification rather than replacement. Something needs to be winnowed out or added on to make them capable of sustaining reader interest long enough to capture the positive attention of an editor or an agent.

Let's face it—editors and agents read a lot of dreck. In my own experience, more of these rejectable submissions are mediocre than terrible. As I've pointed out, the mandate of the publishing professional is to acquire or represent work that will attract large numbers of readers. That's what we, as authors, want as well, to sell stacks of books we've written. Too many authors sabotage themselves by creating protagonists that are okay but not exceptional.

I began my editing career working with mystery novels. This

genre is unique because the main character of a murder mystery has a heavy burden to carry. The most hideous of crimes is committed. A life is taken, disrupting the balance of the universe of the story. The protagonist must restore that balance. To accomplish this task, she'll have to be what I described in secret number six as "a person of substance, complex enough to command and hold reader attention from dramatic opening page to satisfying ending."

One novel that was recently submitted to me illustrates the exact opposite of the effective murder mystery protagonist I just described. In the novel, the close friend of the protagonist, Sarah, is brutally murdered. Her friend was a good woman who, even as she expired, managed to be helpful and leave a last-breath clue. Unfortunately, no one takes that clue seriously, not the police or the victim's family or Sarah. Mystery readers expect a sleuthing protagonist to be sharp-eyed, intelligent, and inquisitive. Such a protagonist would never fail to follow up on an unexplained clue. Sarah dithers past the point, not just once, but again and again. She may be appealing in other ways, but she's too much of an airhead to carry the story.

In commercial fiction, a story must focus on a character most readers will admire. A character who does stupid things, or fails to do smart ones, eventually incurs our disrespect. The less we respect her, the less we care what happens to her. She's lost reader appeal. Which doesn't mean she can't screw up ever, but only once, or maybe twice, and always because dire story circumstances drive her to it. After which, she gathers her wits about her and corrects the damage she's done.

What about the character in the process of becoming ? He needs more development, and it shows. The author doesn't yet know the character well enough to be writing him. A good example of this can be found in another manuscript critique featuring a hero named Ray. We learn that Ray is recently divorced and shy of getting emotionally involved again, but that's all we really know about him. The author seems to be holding back. I happen to know he's doing that because this story is somewhat autobiographical. This protagonist is really the author.

You might think this an advantage. We need to know Ray better, and so does the author. Since Ray *is* the author, that should be a piece of cake, right? Wrong! This author is too close to his subject to see him objectively. He's too emotionally involved. He is also hesitant to reveal too much about himself, or perhaps that territory is too painful for him to explore just yet. When choosing a real-life role model for a fictional character, the self is often the worst choice. Not so, however, of an aspect of the self, a part of you specific enough to define, then explore both in-depth and at some distance. Use the exercise in the crossroads section of the first passage to select the aspect of your life that could enrich your character.

When portraying this aspect of yourself, stick to concrete scenes rather than introspection and rumination, which can slow your story pace disastrously. Treat this character as if he were a total fabrication, because, in some respects, he is. Research and develop him as you would any other character. Detail his past life in order to give him authentic present life on the page. In the fourth passage of this book, I present my character development technique, which you can use to get to know your characters.

Finally, there's the character we simply don't believe. At the outset of her story, Amanda is portrayed as a wimp. She can't manage her life. She comes across as ineffectual, even cowardly, until a calamity occurs and Amanda is suddenly transformed into a powerful aggressor. I'm not saying that this can't happen in a story, but the author must first convince us that it could by motivating the character adequately. Amanda, in essence, steps into a phone booth as a cipher and emerges as Superwoman—and we're not buying that metamorphosis. Maybe we would if we understood not just how it happened, but why it happened.

Secret #8: Never Shortchange Motivation

To create the hero a reader will buy and not want to throw away afterward, think about what that reader's character preferences might be. Most of us prefer to read about a can-do/will-do character. Most readers identify with a bold, active response to the kind of trouble and conflict a protagonist must be in to make a story dramatic and compelling.

A bold character makes herself vulnerable, exposes herself to scary possibilities, because that's what decisiveness in her story situation requires. Still, she is human. She has no superpowers. We care about her because she's like us, not vastly superior to us. Still, we believe she can perform as she does in the story situation because the author lets us in on the character's reasons for doing so. Failing in that authorial duty is a huge storytelling mistake.

In another manuscript I received, Hank's creator does him good service in terms of making him strong. He's no wimp like Amanda started out to be. Yet, we don't believe his behavior any more than we believed hers. A single incident makes him angry. He takes off on a hell-bent trajectory, which he sticks to like glue through the entire story regardless of consequence or danger. The strong, right-thinking Hank we meet at the beginning of the story should eventually rise above this slight. We don't accept that he would put himself, and others, through a heap of hassles for the reason his author provides.

To understand why the author takes this particular wrong turn with his story, we need to examine his own motivation. He needed an incitement, a kick in Hank's hindquarters to get him moving into the story action. This author apparently grabbed at the first thought that came along, which is just about always a poor storytelling decision. Further, deeper thinking could have produced more plausible results. This author has written and published many books for which he created many strongly motivated characters. Nonetheless, no author can afford to settle for convenient, contrived plotting and characterization at any point in his career.

Another motivator too weak to carry us very far is curiosity. For example, in another submitted manuscript, Renee, our protagonist, alienates her best friend by asking impertinent questions for no better reason than what is presented as idle curiosity. We're never taken inside Renee's mind to see her good reasons for this upsetting interrogation, if indeed she has them. Renee is the narrating character, and inside her mind is exactly where we should be. Instead, she appears to behave arbitrarily, even maliciously. We dislike her for that, which weakens her as a protagonist with reader appeal.

In another story, when Brad's situation creates a desperate need for him to take action, he declines because he's afraid of losing emotional control, of getting too involved. Such reasoning can work for a protagonist under limited circumstances, generally at the beginning of his story, but not for the entire book. This motivation is neither strong enough nor admirable enough to dictate the behavior of a supposedly heroic character, especially when extreme consequences are at stake. Again, we believe he'd get over it before many chapters have passed.

Once more, additional imagining is needed. In place of Brad's self-absorbed inner conflict, or at least in addition to it, the author must create real external conflicts between Brad and the other characters that make him legitimately reluctant to act. Even so, he'll have to be intensely, passionately, dramatically driven from the scene by these conflicts before we sympathize with his aversion to getting involved.

"The nobler the motive, the more interesting the story," says John Gardner, author of *The Art of Fiction*. Brad's author might take him in that direction and give him a high-minded, selfless, moral reason for doing what he does, or for not doing what he doesn't do. This works as a storytelling choice because the nobler the motive, the more significant the struggle. Not only does the character have substance as a person, his behavior has substance in the world at large. Struggle, an even more resonant term for conflict, intensifies a story, especially moral struggle.

Mystery author Elmore Leonard speaks of more personal motivations, but his words ring equally true. He says that every person wants the same thing—to get what will make him happy. His criminal protagonists don't think of themselves as criminals. They do what they believe they must to get along. We may not find these motivations admirable, but we recognize their credibility. We also do what we must to get along, though most of us keep our life choices within the limits of the law. It takes a writer as gifted as Leonard to carry off a protagonist with motives most readers disrespect.

To make your story intense, your protagonist must want something intensely, something she absolutely must have or have happen. The more desperately she wants/needs this thing, the more dramatic your story will be. Her intensity gives critical urgency to your story. What she wants is significant, preferably to others as well as herself. If she fails, dire circumstances will result. Her desire and need are contagious. We contract that contagion. We believe in her feelings because her intensity makes us feel the same. She may not start out the story with this desire. It may even be forced upon her, but she embraces it as her own. We, as readers, do the same.

We must, however, comprehend clearly what she desires and why. Clarity is more readily achieved when your protagonist has a single major motivation, one goal she absolutely must attain. Make this desire clear-cut, definite, straightforward, and tangible. Abstract, purely philosophical or ideological motivations often lack emotional resonance. They don't hook a reader at feeling level, where it counts.

A great story has decisive characters. They pursue their decisions with forceful energy powered by their desire. This desire makes them into compelling personalities fueled by passionate commitments, even if they weren't at the beginning of the story. Anything less falls short of a great story. Anything less falls short of your own desire to create a story the reader won't want to put down. Anything less sets your story hook too shallowly in your reader for true emotional involvement to occur. All of which begins with motivation, the "why" of everything your character does.

Secret #9: Build a Hero We Look Up To

I've already pointed out how Elmore Leonard refutes the heroes-should-be-heroic rule with great success. Perhaps the secret of that success is the realism of the characters he creates. Whatever extraordinary things they may end up doing, they are, in general, very ordinary people. As Leonard says, they wake up each morning thinking about what they'll wear that day, the mundane details of life, just as most of us do. Another secret of their success may be the jaded nature of our times.

Patricia Highsmith published her Tom Ripley series in an earlier, less favorable cultural climate. Tom is anything but heroic. His story adventures are, nonetheless, gripping from beginning to end. Until recently, however, they were more cult favorites than box office successes. Highsmith moved to France, in part, because she'd failed to find a wide American audience.

As a protagonist, Tom is definitely one of the sharper knives in the drawer. He simply applies that cutting edge in dastardly ways. Even in his recent film incarnation as *The Talented Mr. Ripley*, I believe we are more aghast at the pervasiveness of his sociopathy than attracted by it, regardless of how cynical today's audience may be in comparison with the 1956 readership Highsmith confronted at first publication of this story. I also suspect that even this film wouldn't have been as well-received without boy-next-door type Matt Damon playing Ripley. Previous casting of bad-boy-next-door type Dennis Hopper as Tom in Wim Wenders' *The American Friend* (an adaptation of Highsmith's *Ripley's Game*) made far fewer American friends.

Despite the popularity of these two exceptional authors in the contemporary marketplace, or maybe because of that exceptionality, I continue to assert the following: If your goal is wide audience appeal, go with the admirable, preferably heroic hero. I base this assertion on two things. First, the best-seller lists. Check out *The New York Times Book Review* lists. Almost all of the fiction titles you find there tell the story of an admirable protagonist confronting great obstacles in an admirable way. Second, my experience as editor and literary agent concurs.

Caroline is the protagonist of a historical romance novel set in early nineteenth-century England. We're told she's a woman of spotless character, which would be an appropriate portrayal if it were borne out by her behavior. Readers of this genre prefer their heroines intelligent, wise, and, above all, dignified. Such a heroine would never join a traveling company and perform for a procurer in a risqué tableau. That's what Caroline does, and not for strong enough motives to make her actions acceptable. She's a married woman, though unhappily so. She is also a member of the landed gentry who has considerable financial means. She doesn't need to disgrace herself and her family to escape her husband. To make matters worse, Caroline allows herself to be treated in a degrading fashion on more than one occasion.

A Regency period heroine may find herself in dire straits and approach crises in many ways, but never at the expense of dignity and self-respect. Otherwise, she becomes too tawdry to qualify as a heroine for this genre. Caroline's creator gives us a main character of questionable judgement, even by contemporary standards. Plus, she disregards the conventions of her genre. Regency novelist and my former client, Jo Beverley, disregards the same conventions with much different results. Her characters are spirited, strong, inventive, and often irreverent, but are motivated in ways contemporary readers understand and support.

In Sebastian's case, I wonder if even his author liked him very much. He describes his protagonist as "cold and distant and uncaring." Aloofness and lack of compassion would have to be counterpointed by some pretty noble qualities to turn Sebastian into an attractive personality. That can be an interesting characterization, for a hero in particular—remote on the surface with depths to be discovered underneath. But beneath Sebastian's craggy surface beats a heart of pure stone, with no reason even approaching nobility for his hardness.

Kendra, on the other hand, has heroic qualities but is never called upon to use them. Her story is meant to be suspenseful. To be the center of that suspense, she should be in danger, real danger that might even threaten her life. She's initially presented as a strong person, resourceful, and brave. We, as readers, are eager to see those strengths tested by extreme circumstances. Unfortunately, those circumstances never arise.

The author could have made more effective storytelling choices. She could have concocted a perilous situation, perhaps an accident that Kendra only narrowly escapes. Better still, another character, preferably somebody vulnerable, like a child, could encounter serious threat. Kendra risks her own safety to rescue that other character. Either of these scenarios would reveal her admirable nature in action and intensify the pace of the story. But no such scenarios occur. Kendra is a heroine waiting to happen. The author has squandered the dramatic potential of her protagonist and her story.

Secret #10: Don't Disrespect Heroics

This book is about writing fiction for the commercial marketplace. More specifically, it is about writing fiction with a chance of reaching the commercial marketplace instead of being rejected along the way. That is my primary theme. My secondary theme has to do with taking power over what happens to you in the publishing business. These two themes meet at the juncture of choice. No storytelling choice is more pivotal than the one that answers the question, "Who is your protagonist?"

Making this characterization choice is one way of taking power over your chances in the publishing marketplace. One choice increases your chances of acquisition by a mainstream publisher. Another choice diminishes those chances significantly but doesn't necessarily destroy them altogether. You take power when you consciously decide on which side of that line to take your stand. Whatever the outcome, you've made your own choice with your eyes wide open and your reasoning well-founded. First, however, you need to understand the lay of the land on each side of that divide. I shall focus on what I consider to be the more-chances side. You can extrapolate from there.

When I speak of commercial potential, I'm talking about sales. What kind of protagonist sells? The protagonist who sells best is the protagonist who appeals to the most readers. What qualities should that character have to appeal to a large readership, the audience editors and literary agents are concerned about reaching? What qualities would be unappealing to the majority of contemporary readers?

Characters are the means by which a reader identifies with a story. This identification breaks down the barrier between words on a page and living images in the reader's psyche. The reader begins to care what happens to the characters. Thus, they are transformed into something beyond mere characters, closer to real people in the reader's mind. The reader is developing an emotional response to the story. He desires a certain outcome for a given character and dreads its opposite. His investment in the story mounts. He's hooked, and that is where any author wants a reader to be.

The protagonist is the pivot point for this identification process. If our goal is to maximize commercial potential, we should design a protagonist with maximum reader identification potential. This character's goals and desires are admirable in terms of nearly universal, right-headed values. These goals and desires are clearly presented, straightforward, and easy to understand. Most readers will identify with such a character and experience empathy toward her. Empathy means being able to feel the feelings, think the thoughts, and share the attitudes of the character.

We identify with the empathetic protagonist because she is what we aspire to be and hope we already are, if only in our better mo-

ments. She is likable in a number of ways. She behaves rationally
and doesn't make stupid decisions, except in extreme and mitigating
circumstances, because almost nobody likes a fool. She isn't weak
and doesn't wait passively for things to happen to her, because almost nobody likes a wimp. She seizes initiative and takes strong,
logical action to deal with obstacles and problems.

On the other hand, the empathetic protagonist is neither Super-
man nor Superwoman. A character who always succeeds quickly
eliminates any possibility of suspense in the story. We can predict
he will overcome whatever he faces. Predictability eliminates the two
questions that keep us turning pages: What happens next? and How
will all of this turn out? The too-perfect protagonist fails in reader
identification terms as well, because almost nobody likes a know-
it-all. The empathetic protagonist makes understandable mistakes
but learns from them. He also gets himself out of whatever hot
water those mistakes may have thrown him into.

The ultimate empathetic character is not only concerned with his
own fate. Love is the emotion readers find most compelling in fiction,
as in real life. He is not, however, a bleeding heart, overly sentimental
and mushy. He cares about someone other than himself in the story,
and he's willing to put himself in physical or emotional jeopardy to
help that other character. This willingness to sacrifice makes this protagonist more than empathetic. It makes him heroic.

What is heroic, anyway? A larger-than-life protagonist is called
upon to be heroic in the larger world—his community, his profes-
sion, his society, his country, the world, maybe even a world of
fantastical dimensions. The ordinary-person protagonist is called
upon to be heroic in the personal, private realm—most often impact-
ing his relationships. Both of these characters, each in his respective
sphere, stand up for what is right and just. Such a character acts

on behalf of this rightness and takes risks accordingly. He does what has to be done, though perhaps reluctantly, and finds within himself the courage necessary to take action, whether he previously recognized that courage in himself or not.

Think back to Caroline, our inappropriate Regency protagonist who joins a risqué traveling company. What might we do to make her into a proper heroine of her genre? First, we unmarry her. She has more latitude, even in Regency England, as a single woman. Next, let's make her a widow, maybe of that era's Napoleonic Wars. Or, maybe we want to justify her behavior now, but cause her more trouble and conflict down the road, so we falsely inform her she's a widow and have her husband show up later on in the story.

Meanwhile, she's in dire straits. Preferably, someone who depends on her is also imperiled. She's tempted, by selflessness, not desperation, to resort to the degrading alternatives the present Caroline chooses. It doesn't take our Caroline long to reject that direction. In its stead, she uses her ingenuity, plus her strength of character, to come up with another way out of her predicament. This way is more personally risky and difficult, but she's determined to triumph and struggles to that end.

In another example, how can we fix cold, aloof, uncaring Sebastian? He must travel a very different road toward reclamation. How about the type of revision previously suggested? Beneath his unapproachable exterior, he is actually an affectionate, generous man, too much so for his own good. He has credible, substantial reasons for his pretense. He's not just in a pout because somebody, probably a woman, once upon a time hurt his teensy feelings. He has, perhaps, been shut down emotionally by great grief and loss. Something that takes place in this story situation, preferably involving the dire need of another character, prompts him to move, gradually and believably, beyond his protective masquerade of non-caring and straight into the reader's heart.

In our third example, Kendra, the heroine waiting to happen, requires little or no rewrite as a character, but her plot needs a makeover. Crucial circumstances must arise, forcing her to make difficult and critical choices. Those choices put her in harm's way—physically or morally. Her innate intelligence, independence, and determination are sorely tested. In response, she acts rather than allowing herself to be acted upon. She gets into trouble, then drags herself out of it. Whether or not she prevails in the end, she proves herself, along with our reincarnated Caroline and Sebastian, becoming a heroine we can look up to at last.

Crossroads

AN AUTHOR SELF-INTERROGATION

For this Q&A session with your favorite author (yourself), I ask you to do something very difficult. I ask you to interrogate yourself about your protagonist. This is tantamount to requesting a critique of your grandchild. I know this because I am both an author and a grandmother. If anybody so much as suggested to me that my granddaughter required an evaluation, my back would shoot up so high there'd be vertebra imprints on the ceiling. She's perfect. She's wonderful. End of story.

It's almost that hard to be objective about a character you've created. Many times, I've heard authors refer to their books as their babies. I believe it is more accurate to think of characters in those terms, especially your main character. He is the offspring of your imagination. You gave him form and substance. You manufactured his life history. After you've been together a while, this character's heart beats in time with your own, often as loudly as your own, or louder. There are human beings in your day-to-day world—acquaintances, friends, even relatives—who are less real to you than this person you've seen only in your mind's eye.

This creation of yours may frustrate you, vex you, infuriate you, keep you up at night, and tempt you to delete her from the screen or shred every page on which she appears. You admit all of that readily and with some satisfaction. Yet, I strongly suspect you'd be hard-pressed to entertain the slightest possibility that your character could be less than fascinating, marginally interesting, or even—perish the thought—a bit of a bore. You have no doubt whatsoever that your character is strong enough to carry the burden of your story plus a couple of others. Your protagonist is perfect, wonderful. End of story.

Okay, I hear you. I acknowledge your defense of your baby, but the time has come for brutal honesty. You must push beyond your indignation. Stop telling yourself, "What she's saying doesn't apply to my protagonist. Other writers' characters, maybe, but not mine." You must get past that stubborn stance immediately and completely. Otherwise, this interrogation technique and the entire process of self-editing cannot work for you or for your story.

You must think of your protagonist as if someone else created him. He is somebody else's grandchild—smudge-faced, bratty, asking for gifts every time he walks past a store. He is definitely in need of a bath, a lesson in manners, and a load of discipline. If he were your grandson, you'd give him all of that and more. You must cultivate this kind of objectivity toward your characters in order to edit them effectively, especially your main character. At the same time, you must stick close enough to hear the secrets of your character's heart and psyche—secrets he may have kept from you until now because you were too deep under his skin, too identified with him, to hear or see everything about him clearly.

Ask yourself each of the following questions. Answer each fully and honestly, as if this were somebody else's kid, not your own.

1. What does your protagonist want in this story? Is this desire significant enough to make a reader also want it for your character? Is this desire significant enough to make a reader want it for your character through the length of an entire book, as long as the character wants it for herself? Or—does this desire, sooner or later, pale into "Who cares?" territory for the reader?

2. How much does your protagonist want this thing? Is this the most crucial need, or close to it, that this character has ever experienced? Does the reader, in fact, recognize that this character has a life before and beyond this story in order to be able to make this judgment? Will the reader be able to identify with your character's feeling of crisis when it comes to this desire? Have you adequately presented and communicated that atmosphere of urgency? If not, how, specifically (in scenes, action, dialogue), can you turn up the story heat on the intensity of his desire?

3. Why does your protagonist want this thing? Are her reasons (her motivations) admirable? Are her reasons logical in this story situation? Are her reasons believable to the extent that a reader will accept them as strong (substantive, legitimate, urgent) enough to motivate a strong (intelligent, independent, principled) protagonist throughout the entire length of your story? Will a reader not only believe these character motives, but adopt them on behalf of the character and root for the character to achieve her desires?

4. What does your protagonist *not* want? All motivations are not positive. Is your character running away from something? If so, what is it and why is he on the run from it? Is your character avoiding something? If so, what is he avoiding and why? What is your character afraid of? (To up the drama/intensity/power/ ante of your story, every character, especially your main character, should fear something.) Why is your character afraid of this thing? For dramatic purposes, your protagonist should come face-to-face with his fear in this story. How does that confrontation come about? Does your character overcome his fear, or does he not?

5. What is at stake for your protagonist in this story situation? What will happen if she fails to achieve what she wants or needs? Are those consequences dire and dreadful enough to make a reader dread them as well? Who, beyond your main character, will also be (adversely) affected by these consequences, and how pervasive and long-lasting will those effects be? Will a reader care deeply enough about these adversely affected characters to be apprehensive about what might happen to them? How, specifically (in scenes, action, dialogue), can you up the ante yet again, where these stakes are concerned, by making the potential consequences more devastating, pervasive, far-reaching? Brainstorm the possibilities, always pushing yourself beyond the first, most obvious possibility toward less expected, more original ones.

6. What is going to get in the way of your protagonist attaining her desire? How many such obstacles will arise? Are these obstacles progressively more formidable? Do they escalate in urgency, intensity of impact, breadth of consequence? Are these obstacles substantial enough for the reader to believe they could actually impede someone as powerfully motivated as your protagonist?

Brainstorm the possibilities here also. Don't worry about going over the top. Don't even worry about straying into melodrama. You can scale back, if needed, later. Your main worry, as a storyteller, is not about heating the water too hot. Instead, you must make certain not to leave the water too tepid.

Note that, in this sixth phase of your interrogation, you have moved beyond mere characterization into plot. More accurately, you have reached the juncture where plot and character meet. They meet at the point where conflict arises.

Further note that plot elements and conflict situations thus conceived originate from character, which means they are less likely to be contrived and more likely to be organic to the story. Stay tuned for more on that subject in future passages.

POSTSCRIPT TO THIS SELF-INTERROGATION:

These questions are designed to carry you deep into your character, beyond your ego attachment to that character. If a niggling nagging in your gut—and you should pay attention to those cues—tells you that attachment still persists, maybe it's time to find a reader. Be careful that this person has no agenda of his own that might interfere with his objectivity. For example, too much or too little affection for you, or competitiveness with you or your work for any reason.

After this person has read your story, or maybe just your notes for developing your protagonist, ask him the questions in this interrogation regarding that character. Write down what he says. When tempted to contradict or even comment on his comments, bite your lip and keep writing. Don't complain. Don't explain. Listen and record, all the way through. When he's finished, say thank you.

Are You There Yet?

A HANDS-ON EXERCISE

Below, I list what I consider to be the most powerful character motivations and loosely define them. Maybe you can come up with more, but first think about whether or not they might actually be variations of the ones I mention here.

Step One: Choose, from the list below, the single strongest motivation for your protagonist in the story situation you've created. Which of these motivations would produce the most story intensity by causing the most conflict for your character? This may or may not be the motivation you've already selected for your story. This list and the explanations are meant to encourage you to rethink that original choice, test it against these other possibilities, and end up with what is best for your story.

Step Two: For a longer book, or to support the primary motivation when needed, you might want your protagonist to have a secondary motivation, as well—slightly less of a driving force than the primary motivation, but compelling all the same.

Step Three: Give three specific possibilities of how this motivation entered your character's life and came to drive her so passionately.

Step Four: Give three specific examples of how this motivation might emerge and manifest in your story (in possible scenes, action, dialogue).

Step Five: Give three specific examples of how this motivation might cause conflict for your protagonist or further exacerbate conflict that already exists.

Step Six: Repeat steps three through five for your secondary motivation.

THE MOTIVATIONS:

Love: A powerful motivation that can drive a character to his best or worst behavior. This power is intensified, as a storytelling device, because virtually every reader can identify with some aspect of love—the joy of receiving love, the agony of losing love, the poignancy of longing for love.

Self-Preservation: Another powerful motivator is the threat of death. The more imminent that threat, the more intense this motivation becomes, compelling the character to act in ways he may never have considered possible.

Self-Knowledge: Be careful about making this a primary motivation in commercial fiction. It tends to be a bit subtle and inward for that medium. In these stories, the main character should definitely gain self-knowledge, but more as a by-product of what happens to her in the story than as an articulated intention. Just let it happen. Don't belabor it.

Pursuit of Adventure and Life Experience: Don't let this particular motivator make your protagonist behave recklessly, unless you are going to turn that impression around very decidedly and very soon.

Honor and Duty: This motivator is a tough one to make real in contemporary, realistic stories. Beware of the John Wayne syndrome:

Whenever a breach appeared, the character he was playing leapt into it. We tend to distrust or disbelieve such behavior these days. We think of such a character as looking for trouble, neurotic, or just a foolhardy buffoon. If you use honor and duty as a motivator, it needs to be accompanied by some other powerful drive that makes the character's behavior more credible and acceptable.

Avarice: All motivations are not honorable or noble. This is one of those. For that reason, you might not want to consider it as fueling your (preferably) admirable protagonist. If you do choose to portray her as powered by greed, you'll have to find additional motivators and do some deft writing to pull it off. Otherwise, wide reader appeal could be seriously compromised.

Revenge: This motivator is another tricky one—powerful and believable for sure, but unattractive. Even a character intent upon avenging a wrongful death is contemplating a heinous act of his own, unless he only wishes to bring the villain to legal justice. Speaking of villains, they also must be very strongly motivated. These less attractive, more ignoble motives work well for villains, as can the more positive motivators when applied with an evil twist.

Passage 3

WHO'S ALONG FOR THE RIDE?

Your protagonist, like all of us, lives in a larger world beyond herself. She lives in the world of your story. That world, in almost all cases, is populated by other people, other characters. These are generally referred to in writing parlance as secondary characters. That designation can lead to confusion. I prefer to borrow a term from the film medium and call them supporting characters. They support both your protagonist and her story.

I've made a big fuss about your main character. I've emphasized how he drives the story and must have a powerful motivation engine to keep him moving at a compelling pace for the duration of his narrative journey. I've shown you specific examples of flawed protagonist characterizations and how to reimagine those portrayals. Now, to that emphasis on the protagonist, add the consideration that no matter how substantial and fully realized your main character may be, if his supporting cast is weak, the story structure will teeter and topple anyway. To be exact, your manuscript will slide off the editor's desk straight into the return-to-sender pile. The magic dimension number is three, for the protagonist and for the rest of your story folks as well.

Secret #11: First Thoughts for the Second Banana

Your hero encounters a full cast of individuals as she moves through the world of your story. These individuals vary in importance, both to her and to the story. Let me establish right now, however, that I don't approve of functionaries—characters who walk on, perform a mundane task or function, then are never seen or heard from again. If someone opens a door for the main character, I want that person, with or without that door, to appear again in the story in some meaningful way. Perhaps she blocks the protagonist's way, literally or figuratively, in their next meeting. She is purposeful to the story. She supports. She isn't just furniture.

Most supporting characters appear more often and figure more prominently in your story than the door-opener does. They perform roles that move the story forward. They affect and amplify the protagonist's role. A supporting character will, in most cases, not be as fully fleshed out as your protagonist. That doesn't mean you, as author, don't need to know this character and imagine him as a flesh and blood individual.

This member of your main character's supporting cast may be her lover, her enemy, her friend, or someone she isn't yet aware of. This person may be in the story to lessen narrative tension or to moderate narrative pacing by making us laugh. She may be in the story to aggravate narrative tension by introducing a further obstacle to the hero's desire. Whatever her purpose, she must live and breathe on the page. She must be carefully written, all the more so because she appears less often. She must deliberately be designed to impact the story situation.

The most effective story cast is headed by a triumvirate: the protagonist, the secondary protagonist, who is her mate or sidekick or foil, and the antagonist or villain. The protagonist leads the story;

the other two support the story. They are the big three, the foundation upon which the story is built. These characters must explore within themselves as they move through the story, two critical questions: What must I do in this story situation? And on which side of the story conflict do I belong?

These questions relate to the motivation of the secondary protagonist and of the antagonist. How the character responds, how she acts at the behest of that response, constitutes the essentials of her role in the story. Figure out the answers to these questions for each of these characters, determine what their resulting actions will be, and you've pretty much defined the characters in your story situation. The arc of each character's development follows the paths he takes in resolving these questions—or in failing to do so.

Sal's author has not asked herself, or Sal, these questions, nor has she endeavored to answer them. Her protagonist, Eleanor, is a strong character, fully imagined and empathetically portrayed. Sal is not. He could add mightily to the story, but he doesn't. This is a mystery novel, where just about any Holmes could use a Watson, so under-use of Sal is particularly unfortunate. Had the author included Sal more prominently in Eleanor's investigation of the murder, Sal could have provided new possibilities for detection less credible for Eleanor alone. The story also has a problem with too little dialogue and too much inner monologue. Sal also could help with that, by giving Eleanor someone to talk to.

For a mystery novel, plot is an even more crucial storytelling component than it is in other genres. Therefore, how about making a plot-based suggestion to Sal's author for realizing his potential? After asking and answering the two essential character questions, brainstorm additional clues to the identity of the murderer that could arise in the course of the story. At least one of these should be a false clue, referred to in mystery lingo as a red herring. Brainstorm (in scenes and action) how Sal might be involved in discovering, investigating, and figuring out, or failing to figure out, each of these clues. Thus, Sal becomes a more substantial character in the story, and the author provides more plot and more narrative tension.

Sal is a good example of why we need a strong second banana—partner, sidekick, mate, or foil—when we already have a ripe and ready first one. His action in the story can add dramatic event. His interaction with Eleanor can provide emotional depth to her character, and to the story, as we see how she behaves in her relationship with him. Sal's more substantive participation in the story situation creates potential for conflict. He and the adversary, or anybody else, can be in conflict. He and Eleanor can and should be in conflict on certain points. Romantic tension, a potent source of interpersonal conflict if there ever was one, also could arise between them.

As author and creator of the world of your story, you must assign a main purpose to each and every supporting character in that story. This purpose is to serve the motives of the main character and to move the narrative forward. In the cases of the other two legs of the big three triumvirate, the secondary protagonist and the adversary, you will do considerable work in developing their characters and roles before you even start writing.

Less prominent characters may be discovered in the course of writing the story. You won't (and probably shouldn't) have a full complement of characters at the beginning of the writing. Some of these characters will arise from the needs of the story and of the big three characters. They are born naturally out of the existing story situation. Some will come to you intuitively, from your writer's imagination, as you discover aspects of the story you hadn't previously imagined.

As each added character arises and demands citizenship in the world of your story, take the time to bring that character to true life on the page. Ask her the two essential questions. What must you do in this story? On which side of the conflict divide do you belong? Brainstorm the answers. Become more imaginative and original with each new idea. Aim for specifics—specific scene, action, dialogue possibilities—and don't forget potential for story conflict.

Secret #12: Flammable Relationships

"What's wrong with this relationship?" sounds like a women's magazine cover banner. Relationship articles are the bread and butter of that market. How to find a relationship. How to fix the relationship you've found. Relationships are also prime reader interest territory for women's fiction, and beyond that category into other fiction. But let's talk about women's fiction for a moment, because if your goal is to have your work accepted by a publisher, you should give more than a passing thought to writing women's fiction.

Approximately 80 to 85 percent of book readers in the U.S. are women. That statistic has remained fairly stable for years. The majority of this female audience reads women's fiction in some form—literary fiction, mainstream commercial novels, category romance—a very large market with editors constantly searching for new authorial voices. Yours could be one of those voices, especially if you can create heartfelt, convincing relationships. Such relationships are the backbone of this strong-selling segment of the publishing marketplace.

The major anchoring relationship of your story centers around your protagonist, but it takes two to tango. She needs another character to relate to. This doesn't have to be a romantic or even potentially romantic relationship. She can be involved in a deep friendship, a parent-child relationship, or a relationship with a sibling, rival, captor, or tormentor. The possible permutations are as many and various as you can imagine.

However, the most popular fictional relationship, evident in numbers of books written and sold, is the relationship between lovers or potential lovers. Readers may be seeking clues for navigating this problematic realm of human interaction. Maybe they are drawn by the tension inherent in a story of two people attempting to love one another in the face of mounting obstacles. Whatever the attraction, here lies storytelling pay dirt. These two characters inevitably conflict, and do so credibly for readers who have most likely experienced a variation of this conflict in their own lives.

Whether or not the connection between two characters is romantic, the other person in the protagonist's relationship exists, to a great extent, for the sake of that protagonist's characterization. He gives her someone to talk to, moving her thoughts out of her head into dialogue, and cuts down on internal monologue, which can slow the pace of the story (a no-no in most commercial fiction). Dialogue appears more active on the page than paragraphs of uninterrupted narrative, and is also more active to the reading consciousness.

This dialogue must be interesting and compelling, never exposition disguised by quotation marks. You can make dialogue interesting by first creating a complex, fascinating story mate and match for your complex, fascinating protagonist. Give this second character opinions and attitudes different from those of your main character. They may be compadres in general, but on occasion they debate, nettle one another, and even openly conflict.

Except in the relationship between protagonist and antagonist, these conflicts are generally variations in attitude rather than violent disagreements. They serve the storytelling purpose of forcing your protagonist to articulate his feelings and beliefs, thus creating another opportunity for the reader to know your protagonist and identify more closely with him. The secondary character in the relationship need not be portrayed quite so sympathetically. She may be a person in the process of becoming, or evolving, with something major yet to learn in life. She may or may not accomplish that goal in this story.

You also may contrast these two characters in more external ways—family, cultural background, life experience, economic and social status, physical appearance. These differences provide potential for fireworks in the relationship. These fireworks may be sexual or nonsexual. In either case, they ignite reader interest and serve your storytelling purpose. In real life, we usually prefer for people to get along. In fiction, such harmony is boring, as was the case in the relationship between Alana and David.

The author is aware that there should be conflict in the relationship to make it interesting, but she misunderstands what storytelling conflict is. She has Alana and David banter back and forth in smart-mouthed, if not exceptionally smart repartee. Alana's banter strays into meanness now and then, potentially jeopardizing reader affection for her character. David, for his part, can be bossy, and we don't like that in him either. However, the greater problem is that there is no real area of substantive disagreement or conflict between them. They may get on each other's nerves, but basically they get along, chapter after chapter, way too long to hold our interest.

Alana allows David to take the initiative while she sits passively by. There's no balance in this relationship, no juxtaposition of equals or even near-equals. Without the tension of worthy opposition, there are no real sparks between them. Weighted down by the wet blanket of their dull, even annoying relationship, the story fatally fails to ignite. Fortunately, there is potential for legitimate contention between them. David is, as I said, bossy. Alana should object

to that, chafe against it, be tempted to turn away from him altogether because of it. She would have to be portrayed as an active
character in order to make such defiance believable.

Secret #13: No Cartoon Villains

I love a good villain. He does so much for a story. He gives the
reader someone to hate and heightens the reader's emotional
involvement and commitment to the story. He gives your hero someone to struggle against. He personifies the conflict. But to do all
this, he must be formidable. Otherwise, your intelligent, active, resourceful protagonist would make short shrift of this adversary and
be on her way. Without a formidable opponent, the story is over
because, when the conflict is resolved, reader interest wanes.

Introduce your adversary early, to get the conflict started right
away. If his identity is a mystery, don't reveal it until near the end
to keep the tension hook set deep in the reader. In a suspense novel,
you may choose to introduce the villain early so we can see firsthand
how formidable he is and recognize his collision course with the
protagonist. She isn't privy to this information and has no idea who
her adversary might be. She only knows she's in desperate trouble,
maybe even physical danger. She may be acquainted with this person
and trust him. Our apprehension for her mounts as she inadvertently
exposes herself to peril, and the story hook is set deeper in our
consciousness with every page.

If that's all there is to it, what's the problem with creating villainous
characters? Patrick embodies a number of those problems. He's also
typical of many of the manuscripts that crossed my desk throughout
the years, inviting rejection as if they wanted it. Patrick's story—or I
should probably say Jacob's story, since he's the protagonist—is gener-

ally well-written. The author has published several other books. He's
mastered the demands of style and voice. He understands how to concoct a plot that holds reader interest all the way through. Nonetheless,
in Patrick he's created what I call the devil-made-him-do-it villain.

Patrick has killed two people so far. We know he's going to kill
more. We suspect already, way too early in the story, what his motivation must be. Patrick is a psychopath or a sociopath or whichever
path his sick psyche compels him to be, and there's the problem. He's
propelled along by his demons, the tormented legacy of his history,
or maybe just a chemical imbalance. He does evil because it's his
nature to do evil, and that's that. He's a scary piece of work for sure,
which is important in capturing reader involvement. A character that
terrifies a reader has him as emotionally invested in the story as a
character that inspires a reader's affection does, maybe more so.

So, what's wrong with psycho Patrick anyway, aside from his
penchant for decapitation or eviscerating in the nude or whatever?
First problem: there are far too many people like Patrick in the real
world and in the writings of aspiring novelists. Patrick could fit
aptly into my later discussion of cliché character. I prefer him here
because he has more reasons to be out of favor with editors and
agents than just his ubiquity.

The prevalence, or what feels like the prevalence, of human
monsters in contemporary real life and tabloid journalism encour-
ages authors to adapt this type into a character. Unfortunately, Patrick and his grisly band of fellow psycho villains are fictionally boring because they don't have an interesting motivation for what they
do. They behave as they behave because they have to, no fascinating
revelations or chilling confessions required. He's a nutcase, end of
story. Which makes him as two-dimensional as Oil Can Harry of
the old black and white cartoons or J.R. Ewing in a later era. The

credits roll over J.R.'s leering grin after he unveils his latest dastardly plan. He does bad things because he gets a kick out of doing them. He is also a cartoonish character.

What makes the difference between a two-dimensional, cartoonish adversary and a credible villain capable of haunting our brain matter as well as our nerve endings? The difference is that we know and understand, on a mentally engaging level, the reasons for an effective villain's behavior. We don't have to sympathize with that behavior, as some writing texts claim, but we must understand it. You, as author, have to conjure for us the genesis of this character's twistedness. That is how you make him real and, thus, scarier than ever.

Also, you must present this person objectively. Your role as author is not to judge your adversary but to give him life on the page, which means you tell his story as he would tell it. That isn't easy for most of us who, compared to Patrick, are grounded in relative emotional normalcy. My secret for getting inside the soul of an evil, or maybe just garden-variety bad character is to tell yourself the following, and believe it: Every villain is the hero of his own story. Think about that for a moment. The most credible, most chilling villain is the one who's convinced his actions are justified because, in the world as he perceives it, they are.

The effective villainous character has motivations that are clear, strong, and believable, but warped. The specific nature of that warp is yours to imagine. Brainstorm those possibilities. Go for the most original option. If you think as your adversary would think, from the perspective of his warped self-righteousness, he will take you to some fascinating territory. Don't be afraid to go there. Such characters are illuminated in dark places. For further guidance along the sociopathic path, I recommend *People Of the Lie* by M. Scott Peck. Talk about a creepy read, and it's nonfiction, too.

Secret #14: Déjà Character All Over Again

I once wished that I'd never be bored. When life turns chaotic, I sometimes think better of that. Still, boredom is something few of us enjoy, especially in our reading. Cliché characters devastate a story's interest level. A character we've seen too many times, more a type than a person, is monotonous at best, infuriating at worst. Imagine how much truer that is for an editor or agent, confronting submission after submission, praying not to be bored, having that prayer go mostly unanswered. The last thing you want to do is cross an editor's desk with a character likely to add to her ennui.

As I said before, I don't approve of functionaries. I like clichés even less. The crusty but benign older gentleman, the doddering but foxy grande dame, the good-hearted prostitute, the down-at-the-heels shamus with a bitter edge. Grab a piece of paper or a note card, and come up with your own additions to this list. These are types known mostly or only for this pairing of characteristics, their two dimensions. They always behave according to that signature. They have no life beyond it, no real history or emotional depth. Any appendages they carry with them—a cat, a predictably broken-down car or house, a relentless peeve—are extensions of that signature. These cliché characters are important because they influence your protagonist's story in some way. Beyond that, they have no existence. There's nothing wrong with that in the hands of a seasoned novelist who can pull it off without producing a story populated by stick figures. Dick Francis can give us an economical description of a secondary character, a simple definition of who and what that character is in the story. In as little as a paragraph, that character is vested with depth and presence. He's more than a cardboard cutout. Yet, the author is never in danger of allowing him to take over the story. Simply put, Dick Francis performs this feat by associating each character, no matter how minor, with an emotional dimension for the main character and the story. In *To The Hilt*—via the voice of his narrator, Alexander Kinloch—he even manages to accomplish that with a character who is deceased:

> My mother's unvarying composure, I sometimes thought, stemmed from a deficiency of emotion. I had never seen her cry, had never heard tears in her voice, not even after her husband, my father, had been killed in a shooting accident on the moors. To me, at seventeen, his sudden loss had been devastating. My mother, dry-eyed, told me to pull myself together.

In this single paragraph, Dick Francis has Alexander's mother pinned down for us for sure. We know who she is and what she is. If we read with discernment, we also can anticipate that the experience of having her as a decidedly non-maternal parent has influenced the kind of man Alexander both has and has not become. We will be alert for those influences as the story progresses—and all from a single, carefully and succinctly, conceived paragraph.

I believe it is idiotic to suggest that, if you give a minor character some resonance and reality, he will get out of hand and dominate the scene. This suggests that an author has no control over what goes on in his work. That is totally untrue. Your story is born and given life in the country of your imagination. You rule that country and are all-powerful at all times. You can alter circumstances any way you wish at any juncture of the story. Believing otherwise diminishes your power as a storyteller. It also lets you off the hook in terms of assuming responsibility for what happens in your story. You exert absolute control over your characters' behavior and the roles they play. You created them; they are yours.

Therefore, you are free to give each secondary character a soul and a life beyond her few scenes in your story. You may tap only brief moments of that life, but they can be real moments, enriching your story and deepening the complications surrounding your main character. Know who each minor character is. Feel her as a living, breathing being. Then, slice off a wedge of that life to insert in your story, at a juncture where this minor character's life encounters the conflicted circumstances of your protagonist and affects those circumstances in some way. If the character you've created ends up with way too much going for her than this story requires, consider giving her a book of her own. In this era of successful sequels, spinoffs, and series, how could it hurt?

In another manuscript submitted to me, an author who could have benefited from this advice created the character of Lucy. Lucy is what you'd call an airhead. That may be a politically incorrect way of describing a woman, but Lucy is worse than politically incorrect in this story. She's cardboard. She isn't very bright. She's overtly sexy in a wide-eyed, supposedly ingenuous way. She's out of control of her life and blunders into more trouble with each passing scene. She waits, like a damsel in distress hanging from a cliff, for somebody to come along and save her bacon. That somebody will, of course, be a man.

Not only is Lucy a cliché, she's out-of-date. For many women and men, she is offensive. This isn't about political correctness. It's about sabotaging your work with editors. This is where common sense comes in. A lot of editors are women. In some categories of publishing, most of the editors are women. You might not submit directly to a woman, but your manuscript will have to pass muster before an editorial board with women on it. The women I've met in publishing tend to be progressive in their thinking, independent and liberated in their behavior. Lucy would not pass muster with them at all.

Nor would the relationship she has with Hatch, the protagonist of this story. With him, Lucy turns into a sex-on-the-brain temptress intent upon seduction, whatever the cost. She forgets about the mortal danger she's in and can focus on nothing other than her lust for our hero. Whose fantasy is this, anyway? Remember what I said about the major percentage of novel readers being women? How do you think that audience would respond to Lucy and Hatch? Sneer? Laugh? Toss the book across the room?

Reed is another character in need of update, though he's not quite as last-century as Hatch and Lucy. Reed is simply a character we've seen way too often. He's what the women's magazines have dubbed a commitment-phobe. His character signature is that he refuses to get into a meaningful relationship with a woman, no matter what. He's been burned in the past, blah, blah, blah. He loves his freedom, blah, blah, blah. The behavior lacks depth and the motivation is too commonplace and shallow. Reed is a cliché.

With some character excavation and re-thinking, Reed could become a three-dimensional man after all. Unfortunately, in my opinion, Lucy and Hatch are beyond reclamation. Let them rest in peace in the rejection pile where they ultimately came to reside.

Secret #15: Take Care to Triage

Who does and does not belong in your story?

Let's make a couple of lists. Following these lists, I offer some specific characterization don'ts. All have been taken from manuscripts that were submitted to me and, subsequently, returned to their authors.

CHARACTERS THAT BELONG IN YOUR STORY
1. They sparkle with contradiction and controversy.

2. They spark off the other characters in the story, especially the main characters.
3. They have secrets the other characters would like to or should know.
4. They have hidden dreams the others would like to or should know.
5. They generate plot.

CHARACTERS THAT DON'T BELONG IN YOUR STORY
1. They don't make anything happen.
2. They get along with everyone, neither creating nor enhancing conflict.
3. We aren't interested in knowing more about them.
4. They are not connected with either the main character or the main character's story.
5. They don't generate plot.

The Lackluster Character—Martha is in the editorial spotlight at full wattage because she's the sleuth in a proposed mystery series. Unfortunately, she is neither unique nor compelling. Any continuing series must have a protagonist who stands out among the very large pack of genre submissions. Too many beginning series writers focus on plot to the exclusion of character. This oversight can be fatal. The series protagonist must be memorable and strongly differentiated from other published characters in the genre.

The Character Who Cloys (or Generally Annoys)—Priscilla is cute enough to kill, which has the alleged hero scampering along in her wake for far too long. At first, she is almost as lovable to the reader as to the hero. Then, we become exasperated with her and, eventually, out and out irritated. She's a distraction from the story, and she undermines our identification with the hero as well.

The Character Who Fails at His Story Mission—Damian is the detective who doesn't detect. A murder is committed. Damian claims to be intent upon finding the murderer but does far too little to further that quest. He avoids real investigative questioning. He is developed as a character but not as a generator of plot. He waits around for others to do the legwork. The activities he does undertake (record searches, etc.) are far too static to spark reader interest. They slow the pace of the story instead of enlivening it. Damian should be the catalyst for dramatic tension. He should thrust himself into serious danger and battle his way out. He does neither. He fails at his story mission.

The Character Who Shocks for Shock's Sake—Hudson is a gross-out character. I won't detail his grossness here because he'd probably have to be expurgated if I did. Suffice to say he has sexual proclivities and anatomical peculiarities that make him repulsive, though possibly erotically stimulating to read about. This character is inappropriate to the genre and the publisher to which this submission was made, and would be to many others. Hudson was created to be shocking, to impress with how daring this author can be. He performs little effective story function beyond his shock value. He not only doesn't add to the story, he detracts from it because, in his grossness, he distracts.

Interchangeables—Davidson is an okay protagonist, but he keeps running into characters who are basically ciphers. They give him information or fail to do so, but none of them is differentiated from the others. They all easily could be interchanged with one another. They are even less than functionaries. Their lack of substance drains the story of vitality. These characters, and their interaction with Davidson, must be rewritten to reveal their individuality.

This is only a sampling of characters that should have been triaged out of stories. Make your own list, maybe even from your own work, but don't be discouraged when you do. There are ways to save these characters from the no-hope heap. You'll find one way to do this in the fourth passage. Remember that every character, like every human being, has a story. It is your job as storyteller to discover that story. How much of it you use in your novel will be determined by the needs of that novel, and the need to bring each of your characters to life on the page.

Crossroads

AN AUTHOR SELF-INTERROGATION

This interrogation involves characters in relationships. Read the questions below. Let your mind and emotions roam free. Record, on audiotape or in writing, the impressions and images you conjure in the course of that roaming. Don't censor yourself. Don't be held back by conventions or inhibitions. Engage all of your senses. Imagine your main character's primary relationship in your story, and respond.

1. What are the circumstances under which these two people first meet in this story situation? Why are they there? How are they feeling, individually, about themselves and their lives as they meet? Make these inward responses from the point of view of only one character at a time.
2. Do they like each other at first meeting? If this is a romantic relationship, keep in mind that love at first sight is hardly ever plausible when written down.

3. Whatever these initial feelings may be, they should have changed by the end of the scene. How do their attitudes toward each other evolve? What happened, or was said, in the scene to bring about this change?

4. How do their true feelings contrast with their actions toward each other? Such contrast gives the relationship tension and adds another level of complexity.

5. What does each character think about this confrontation after it is over? There should be conflict in this internal response. One source of such conflict might be fear. If you create a third character and maybe even a fourth, the main characters will have someone to talk to about each other and their conflicts.

6. What are the circumstances of their next meeting and the next and so on? What are the circumstances of their final encounter? Is this the climactic scene of the story as well? Answer the above questions for each of those encounters.

Are You There Yet?

A HANDS-ON EXERCISE

Go somewhere, anywhere, public and fairly crowded. Sit down in an unobtrusive corner where you can take notes without being noticed too much. Pick a person from the crowd. Write down answers to the first set of questions about this person's physicality. Write down answers to the second set of questions (adapted from the crossroads section of the second passage of this book) about this person's story as you imagine it to be.

THE CHARACTER'S PHYSICALITY

1. What is this person's face like? What makes his eyes, mouth, and other features distinctive?
2. How is this person dressed?
3. What is this person's hair like (length, color, style)?
4. How does this person move?
5. Does this person have any mannerisms? What mannerisms might this person have under other circumstances?
6. What is this person's most significant physical feature?

THE CHARACTER'S STORY

1. What does this person want most in life? How, specifically, is this desire significant enough to make a reader care about it?
2. How much does this person want this thing? Is this the most crucial, urgent need this character has ever experienced? If not, what is the most crucial, urgent need in this person's experience?
3. Why does this person desire this thing so much? Is this person's reasons admirable? If so, why? If not, why not? Are they logical? Are they believable? If so, how? If not, why not?
4. What does this person not want? This person is running away from something. What? Why is this person running from it?
5. What is at stake for this person? What will happen if this person fails to achieve his goal? Make sure the consequences are dire.
6. What could get in the way of this person attaining her goal?
7. What is your emotional response to this person, and why?
8. Could you adapt this person into a character for your own work? Where and how, exactly, would this character fit in your story?

Passage 4

COMPANIONS YOU CAN COUNT ON

What would life be without people? Personally, I identify strongly with place. Still, when I travel from my home in the Pacific Northwest to New York City, where I live part of the year, the first thing I do is look up family and friends. As much as I love the Big Apple, it would be flat and unexciting—well, less exciting anyway—without people I care for. They are my source of human connectedness. Otherwise, the apple would be little more than sauce for me.

This prompts the question: What would life be without people you feel connected to? And, where do we connect with people, and with characters, in a meaningful way? For both the people in our lives and the people in our books, we make connections at the heart. We want our readers to make that connection as well. When they do, storytelling magic happens, and you, as author, have created a world that involves the reader at the deepest level.

Secret #16: Going Deep

First, however, you must make that connection yourself. You must get to the heart of each character you create. Novelist Toni Morrison calls this "going deep." She says that the deeper she goes, the better the writing will be. The heart is the deepest part of a person or a character, but it is often hidden because of fear and secrets and lies motivated by fear.

Like any human being in your daily life, at the outset of your relationship with your characters, they show you only the surface of themselves. You may catch an occasional glimpse of what lies beneath, but little more. You must see far beyond these glimpses to write an affecting and memorable character, especially to write an affecting and memorable protagonist. That means you have to get beneath the surface, past the secrets and lies, despite the fear, and into the heart of the character you're creating. This is what Toni Morrison means when she talks about going deep.

Too many manuscript submissions lack passion and vitality. Editors and agents respond to these manuscripts with phrases like, "This doesn't have that special spark we're looking for," or, my personal favorite, "I didn't love this enough." Both are alternate versions of, "This just doesn't work for me." An author pins such letters to a bulletin board or tapes them to the computer, stares at them and wonders, What in the world does that mean? It means the work fails to come alive on the page, which means the characters don't come alive on the page. They have surface, and maybe a glimpse of something deeper, but nothing more. In my experience, this is the reason for most fiction manuscript rejections, whether or not the editor is able to articulate that.

Strong stories begin with strong characters. I don't believe for a New York minute that there's a chicken versus egg relationship between character and plot. Effective plot grows out of effective characters, not the other way around, and building effective character starts at the beginning—or at a new beginning.

Remember my own failed proposal? My protagonist definitely needs a new beginning. Let's give her one and provide an example of how you might rebirth your characters, as well. With this protagonist, Jessica, I've done what so many writers do in manuscripts that don't pass muster with editors and agents: I've focused on her head and neglected her heart. We learn a lot about what she thinks and remembers. We learn almost nothing about what she feels.

In the scary prologue, we know she's scared. Terrifying things are happening so fast she doesn't have the time or capacity to feel anything but fear. Frightening, shocking experiences keep a person, or a character, at this surface level of single, riveting emotion. This fear focus works in the prologue, which is short, as prologues should be. There isn't page space for delving more deeply into character. Chapter one is a different situation entirely.

In a story with a prologue, the first chapter is really a second opening, not necessarily as spectacular, but equally crucial. The prologue hooks the reader into character and a predicament, usually from the past. Chapter one must hook the reader into character in the present. Something dramatic and compelling must happen here to compel the character to act and to set the story in motion. That something must happen to a character the reader feels at least the beginnings of a connection with.

I didn't know enough about Jessica to have made that connection myself. I'm not talking about the facts of her biographical life or the color of her hair. I'm talking about the facts of her emotional life and the color of her feelings. I knew a girl at fifteen, a flash of her anyway, and a little about the woman she's become almost two decades later. This is nowhere near enough to make her three-dimensional and real to me or anybody else.

What was in Jessica's heart, as opposed to her head, an hour before chapter one opens? Who was she then? I have no idea. She's like someone I met a long time ago then encountered again recently, but only for a moment or two. She's barely an acquaintance, certainly not a friend. Yet, I'm supposed to write a book about her. Whoa, Nellie. I've got some work to do before I begin that ride.

Secret #17: Play the Cautionary Notes

Most of what I know that's practical in life started with my grandmother, Alice Jane Rowland Boudiette. Cautiousness was part of her practicality, not stifling or obsessive, simply sensible. A favorite excursion from Grandma's tall, brown house on West Main Street was to my Uncle Mannie's ice cream shop a couple of blocks away. In the year or so before Grandma passed on, I was finally old enough to walk to Uncle Mannie's on my own. Grandma would tie coins into one of her hand-embroidered white handkerchiefs. Uncle Mannie may have been her son, but she was too proud not to pay.

"Keep your coat buttoned, Lovey," she'd say as I hurried down the front porch steps into the brisk winter weather. "Don't speak to anyone you don't know."

I'd be at the sidewalk by then, turning right toward Uncle Mannie's with visions of maple walnut or butter pecan in my head. If I looked back as I walked away, I'd see Grandma still standing on the porch, one hand in her apron pocket to hold it down from flapping in the wind, the other at her forehead shielding her eyes so she could see me skipping down the street. I didn't need to look back. I knew she was there. I could feel her, reinforcing her words of caution with caring watchfulness. I never felt invaded by that. I felt valued. I hope you will feel the same as I echo Grandma's spirit in a storyteller's version of her precautions. Keep your best imagination buttoned to the task, and don't speak to impulses that might lead you astray.

PRECAUTIONS FOR WRITING CHARACTERS FROM THE INSIDE OUT

Being intimate with anyone, truly intimate—as I was just now with the recollection of my grandmother—involves moving into that person. The more deeply you immerse yourself in that person or character, the more intimate you become. At ultimate intimacy, you become the character in the sense that you experience his feelings as your own. I call this knowing a character from the inside out. Instead of observing your character from the outside, you live his life as if it were your own. Precaution: Don't dismiss this concept as too magical, mystical, or metaphysical sounding for you. My practical grandma would have said, "If it works, it works." Then, she'd want it proven to her, along with a step-by-step how-to. The how-to is called "Writing Characters From the Inside Out," my technique for going deep. The proof will be in the results you achieve from practicing that technique on your own characters. The proof is in the pudding, as Grandma would say.

"Writing Characters From the Inside Out" is important because fiction begins with character. Motivation and plot evolve from there. What kinds of characters do we want to create? For the purposes of my focus on commercial fiction, we want to create characters who will appeal to a wide readership. They appeal because they manifest life beyond the intellectual. They come to breathing, talking, moving life on the page. Writing life into our characters requires something adults call role-playing and children call make-believe.

Precaution: Don't be afraid, just do it. This is a reminder I must also make to myself. I went to a therapist once who told me to pick up a chair cushion, pretend it was my husband and tell him exactly what I thought of him. I never went back to that therapist. I'm not a "let's pretend" kind of gal. My feet are too terra-firma-based for that. But I've seen this technique work over and over again. It could work for Jessica, too. So—okay, I give up—let's pretend.

Besides overcoming your inhibitions about make-believe, you must also dispel the notion that "Writing Characters From the Inside Out" will forfeit any of what I consider to be the fun of writing, jumping right in and banging away at a story, imagination full throttle, rational mind left behind. I'm afraid I'll miss the magic if I do too much calculating up front. I do enough calculating in my real life. I don't want it invading my writing life as well. Precaution: Writing for fun without putting thought into your characters leads to the real-life fact that it is even less fun being rejected. Plus, when I recall the elated expressions on my students' faces as they read the results of practicing this technique, I have to conclude that a little up-front calculation isn't such a drag after all.

You are creating a character in a story you want to have published. Precaution: Always keep in mind that you are not recording real life. You're making up a story that is like real life only it is more believable. This story must be more interesting and more suspenseful than real life. Part of what gives a story its fascination is the way in which it is unlike the usual and expected, the way it contrasts with the everyday experience of most of our lives. These unique specifics constitute the story hook. The stronger, more compelling that hook, the more relentlessly it grabs the reader—and the editor.

I expect you will find this exercise easy, even natural to perform. Final precaution: beware of devaluing this technique because of its simplicity. We tend to be puritans at heart. We believe that if something isn't excruciatingly difficult, it can't be worthwhile. Think again. The most profound principles of life are generally the simplest truths. Your heart is the doorway to becoming your character. You must know and care about your characters before a reader can or will.

Secret #18: Here's the Drill

It was early in my editing career when I first noticed that many of my manuscript turndowns shared this same problem—lack of passion in the writing. My teacher instincts slipped naturally into gear. I'd begun my adult professional life, years before, as a high school English teacher. The appropriate response to a problem in the classroom, and lots of problems in other places as well, is to make a lesson plan. That exercise turned out to be "Writing Characters From the Inside Out," the workshop I've since presented across the U.S. and in Canada.

I couldn't offer individual instruction to the authors of the manuscripts I was rejecting, not at much length anyway. I could, however, take that instruction on the road. I resolved to place the problem of bringing vitality to lackluster fiction at the center of my lectures whenever possible. To do that I needed a lesson—an exercise.

THE JOURNAL APPROACH

I believe in the visceral effect of writing things down. Idea begins in the brain; arm muscles respond; energy courses through fingers, into pen, onto paper, forming sentences. I like the organic rhythm of that. I can feel it. You will too, if you handwrite the following exercise as I urge you to do.

Write in a notebook, using a separate one for each story. Leave several blank pages for each item in the exercise. As you write more deeply into your story, fresh ideas will come to you, further insights into the journal responses. Keep track of these new ideas in the blank pages for each question in the exercise. Record every thought you have, however obscure.

Do this exercise, separately, for each of your big three characters—protagonist, secondary protagonist (mate, sidekick, foil), antagonist—and any other characters you need to know more intimately. Secondary characters require less exhaustive exploration than major characters. Nonetheless, even secondaries benefit from this approach.

Don't expect to come close to completing this entire exercise in one sitting. Do allow at least one hour of uninterrupted time for that sitting. Your writing life depends on it.

THE METHOD

1. Write in your journal notebook, responding to the items in the exercise.

2. Write only in the first person, using "I."

3. Write only *as* your character, one character per exercise. You *are* this character. You are not just telling us *about* your character. You are *being* your character and speaking with this character's voice from this character's experience of life.

4. Concentrate on how you, as your character, are *feeling* about each exercise item, and how it relates to you and your life history. Answer from your *gut*, as this character, rather than from your head. Avoid rumination, theorizing, and abstractions.

5. Be specific in your responses as this character. Record scenes (action, dialogue, description) wherever possible. The more dramatic, the better.

6. Don't be daunted by the length of the exercise. Plan on returning, again and again.

7. Fill in the first item, "My Basic Biographical Data," writing as your character.

8. Read through the rest of the items. Mark those items to which you, as your character, have a strong emotional response—either you can't wait to start writing on this subject or you'd prefer never to write about it at all.

9. Read back through *only* the marked items. Mark a second time those items with the highest degree of emotional charge for you, as your character.

10. Put down your pen, and prepare your psyche for the exercise.

PREPARING YOUR PSYCHE FOR THE EXERCISE

It is important to quiet yourself before you move from the intellectual activity of reading on to the more intuitive activity of "Writing Characters From the Inside Out." You are going to travel into something of a light meditative state. Then, you will write for a minimum of one hour of uninterrupted time.

Sit up straight in your chair and close your eyes. Place your feet flat on the floor. Rest your hands comfortably in your lap. Breathe deeply with your mouth closed. Inhale and exhale through your nose only. Inhale to a long count of four; hold your breath in for two counts; exhale to a long count of four; hold your breath out for two counts.

As you inhale, focus on breathing in peace. Focus on breathing in confidence. Focus on filling your body with strength. Know that what you write in this session will be good and will be what you are meant to express at this time.

As you exhale, focus on breathing out tension. Focus on breathing out the concerns of your daily life. Focus on breathing out all doubt about yourself and your work. Know you are meant to be where you are, doing what you are about to do.

Complete several of these long, centering breaths. Feel where the breath is taking you—into silence, into silence, into silence.

With your eyes still closed, begin repeating softly to yourself, "I am (use your character's name)." Repeat this several times, going deeper with each repetition.

Gradually, as you are ready to do so, open your eyes and begin to write in your journal notebook, starting with the first double-marked item on your exercise list.

THE EXERCISE

I. My basic biographical information:

My full name is _____.

I was born in (place name) _____.

My heritage is (racial, ethnic) _____.

The other places I have lived are _____.

II. My additional biographical information:

My birth (or adoptive) family's financial situation was. . . .

Because of that, my attitude toward money is. . . .

My family's status in the community was. . . .

My birth (or adoptive) family consisted of. . . .

The member of my family I am closest to is

_____, because. . . .

The member of my family I am most distant from is

_____, because. . . .

Other than these, my favorite relative is

_____, because. . . .

Other than these, my least favorite relative is

_____, because. . . .

As a child, I would describe myself as. . . .

The most significant experience of my childhood was. . . .

As an adolescent, I would describe myself as. . . .

The most significant experience of my adolescence was. . . .

My first sexual experience was. . . .

My attitude toward the opposite sex has been that. . . .

My educational background is. . . .

My general health is. . . .

My specific health concerns and problems have been. . . .

III. **My physical characteristics:**

What I like about the way I look is. . . .

What I hate about the way I look is. . . .

I believe that other people think I look. . . .

My style of dress is. . . , because. . . .

IV. **My general character traits:**

If you ask me what I'm like as a person, I'd say I'm. . . , because. . . .

I would describe my habits (neatness vs. sloppiness, etc.) as. . . .

I would describe my religious attitudes as. . . .

I would describe my political attitudes as. . . .

I would describe my attitude toward life in general as. . . .

V. **My outstanding character traits:**

The most significant thing I've ever discovered about myself is. . . .

The situation in which I made this discovery happened like this. . . .

I feel that my greatest talent is. . . .

The thing I believe in most strongly is. . . , because. . . .

The thing I care most about in life is. . . , because. . . .

The thing I enjoy, or have enjoyed, most in my life is. . . .

The thing I dislike most in life is. . . , because. . . .

My most important goal in life is to. . . , because. . . .

VI. **My personal history:**

My marital status is. . . .

My experience with romantic or sexual relationships is. . . .

My current attitude toward such relationships is. . . , because. . . .

I have worked in the following jobs. . . .

My feeling about my current work is. . . , because. . . .

My future professional ambitions are to. . . .

My favorite hobby or leisure time activity is. . . . because. . . .

My best friend ever was. . . , because. . . .

My current best friend is. . . , because. . . .

My current place of residence is. . . I like or dislike it there because. . . .

VII. **My emotional history:**

I am most inhibited in the area of. . . , because. . . .

I am superstitious about. . . , because. . . .

I have a phobia about. . . , because. . . .

My greatest disappointment in life is (or was). . . , because. . . .

My greatest frustration in life is (or was). . . , because. . . .

My greatest regret in life is (or was). . . , because. . . .

The time in my life I was most enraged was. . . , because. . . .

The time in my life I was most terrified was. . . , because. . . .

The time in my life I was most humiliated was. . . , because. . . .

The time in my life I was most heartbroken was. . . , because. . . .

The time in my life I was most excited was. . . , because. . . .

The time in my life I was most joyful was. . . , because. . . .

My deepest fear in life is. . . , because. . . .

My darkest secret is. . . , because. . . .

The biggest lie I ever told is. . . . I told it because. . . .

The thing I yearn for most in life is. . . , because. . . .

Secret #19: Tips From the Trip

THE AFTER-THE-EXERCISE EXERCISE

You've exercised for your brain and your imagination; now give your body a little of the same. Stand up and stretch. Arms over your head, hands toward the ceiling. Shake out your legs. Shake out your whole body. You've worked hard. You deserve congratulations. Maybe you had trouble carving out that uninterrupted time or even finding a corner uncluttered enough for writing. You did it anyway. So, congratulate yourself. Stretch your arms overhead once more, bend them back and down. Pat yourself on the back and say, "What a good writer am I. What a good writer am I." Once more, with gusto. "What a good writer am I!"

HANG ONTO IT BY SHARING

My experience has been that, at the end of the "Writing Characters From the Inside Out" exercise, the vast majority of workshop participants were happy, even overjoyed. I trust that, despite doing the exercise from a book, you also were able to capture the spirit of the process and the exuberance of the accomplishment as well.

I encourage you to share the experience. Affirm that experience by speaking about it aloud or writing it down. If communicating aloud, you should do so with someone who also has experienced the exercise. Whenever possible, do the exercise with your critique group or with several writers of your acquaintance.

Have one of the group members explain the exercise method. Have another member lead the light meditation preparing the psyche for the writing. After performing the exercise, each of you shares what you felt about the experience, one at a time. Tell what your emotions were, what it felt like to work on your character this way.

Be free to say whatever is true for you, positive or negative.

If there is no one to join you in the exercise and no one to swap feelings with afterward, turn to your writer's journal. Make this journal your compadre, a place where you confide your wishes, dreams, lies, fears, betrayals, etc., as they relate to your writing and your writing life. Trust your journal with your deepest thoughts. After the "Writing Characters From the Inside Out" exercise, describe your reactions and impressions in your journal pages. Focus on your gut, rather than your head, as you did in the exercise.

If you think this is a one-sided activity, with you giving all the input and receiving nothing in return, think again. You'll find your characters talking back to you as you record your experience with them. They will reveal secrets they've been keeping from you and confess lies they've told and why they told them. Don't worry. You're not losing your mind. That mind is simply thinking, and imagining, as a writer's mind should.

If you're in a group, listen to what other writers experienced. Remember that everyone's response is valid. Write it all down in your writer's journal. Numerous workshop participants report that the exercise is freeing. They began to write in the character's voice, and the words simply flowed. So did the surprises. Details and insights, entirely new aspects of character and character history were revealed.

WHERE'S THE CONFLICT?

In preparation for upcoming passages on plotting, I suggest you follow-up on the "Writing Characters From the Inside Out" exercise. Read back through your responses to the exercise items. Indicate, in colored ink, anything you've written about your character that could lead to story conflict. Also, mark sections that, according to your writer's intuition, need deeper exploration at a later time. Trust

that intuition to tell you the truth about your story, and to keep
you on track toward creating the most vibrant and alive characters
you've ever imagined. Conflict, swirling around your characters and
within them, enhances that vibrancy.

AVOIDING THE BENDS: SECRETS OF GOING DEEP

After doing the exercise, I'd learned some things I hadn't previously
recognized. I share those insights with you here.

1. When responding to the childhood section of the exercise, you
   may find yourself slipping into a child's voice as you write. Go
   where that voice takes you.

2. Responding to the items about your character's parents, a grand-
   parent may appear in that role. Be open to including extended
   family members, or non-blood relations who served a significant
   parenting or sibling role, in your character's history.

3. The exercise should help you understand more clearly than ever
   that your character's story must have something extraordinary
   about it: intense emotion, passion, tragedy, joy, conflict—life at a
   high pitch. Also, be reminded that editors these days are looking
   for intense, larger than daily life, emotionally-charged stories.

4. Some pieces of your character's story may not be clear to you even
   after the exercise. Brainstorm these unclear areas in your next exercise session.

5. Repeat the exercise for each of your big three characters—protagonist,
   secondary protagonist, antagonist—before you proceed with writing
   the book.

6. Finally, your character's responses to the exercise items should reveal
   what she says, thinks, and feels about herself. Consider what other
   characters might think about her. What contrasts would there be

with her self-perceptions? Such contrasts could be sources of story conflict. Add questions to your notebook soliciting these answers.

Secret #20: Final Thoughts on Character

CONTRIVANCE AND CONNIVANCE

If you always begin with character in situation rather than the other way around, you should never end up with a plot that has the feeling of being rigged to suit the author's story needs. The editorial ear and eye are tuned to detecting that sort of thing. Your manuscript will come sailing back at you like a missile aimed point-blank at your publishing career. Never have your character behave in behest of your story needs rather than out of that character's own nature and natural motivation. If you don't truly understand your character's nature, then you need to return to the "Writing Characters From the Inside Out" exercise for more and deeper work. Plot must emerge from character. That's the rule. Break it at your own peril.

SURPRISE US IN EXPECTED WAYS

To prevent your character from being predictable, figure out how your character should behave in a particular situation, as dictated by what you've learned about this "Writing Characters From the Inside Out" exercise. Write that down. Figure out what behavior would be contradictory to this expected one. Write that down. This behavior would be a story surprise. It might even twist the story in invigorating ways. But, this behavior must be made to fit the character. Ask yourself, as the character, "Why am I acting like this?" Remember that the roots of present behavior originate in past history. Go back to the exercise for this character. Find an exercise item where you can create a piece of character history that connects emotionally with what is happening in the scene you are writing. Plan to off-handedly interject this piece of past experience into the story preceding this scene as if you are planting a clue in a mystery.

Crossroads

AN AUTHOR SELF-INTERROGATION

Never forget you are writing to be read, to have your words experienced by others. Part of editing your work is editing that experience. How will your work sound to someone reading it? Does your meaning come across the way you intend it to? Does your voice ring true? Ask yourself these questions at all stages of the writing, beginning right here, at the preparatory stage of building character.

Select a piece of your writing in need of further work. Read over what you've written—the segment, the chapter or, in this case, your exercise responses. Be objective. Ask yourself what *feels* like it doesn't yet say what you want to say in the way you wish to say it. Recognize this as a phase of editing, not a condemnation of your work. Next, you are going to employ the reading-as-critique technique to make your writing stronger. This technique involves reading your work aloud to an actively listening audience. Ideally, this audience will be a person other than yourself, but only if this person meets certain criteria. This listener need not be a writer, though that can help, as long as the writer (or any potential listener) doesn't have an agenda contradictory to your own—a personal reason to bring you down or, oppositely, a personal reason to build you up. Be hard-nosed and realistic in these determinations.

If you have no one available who fulfills these requirements, you will have to be your own audience. This perhaps, demands the greatest degree of hard-nosed realism. You will have to get past your ego, past your emotional attachment to your work. This is not an easy thing to do, but the success of your work depends on it. Make this into a true listening experience by reading your work aloud into a tape recorder. Recast yourself in the role of the active listener as you play back what you have read.

Active listening means you, or your audience, are engaging your entire mind in the experience. You are not listening to be entertained. You are listening, or asking someone else to listen, for the purpose of making yourself a better writer, especially in terms of writing with dramatic impact at the emotional/feeling level of your story. You or your designated audience, while listening, must be thinking of the questions listed below. Have them written out for taking notes during the reading/listening session. As for the reading itself, do your best to be relaxed. Read slowly, clearly, and audibly. Resolve that this will be a learning experience rather than a judging one.

THE QUESTIONS:

1. Do we care about the character in this scene/segment? What specifically *makes* us care about her? What positive qualities does this character exhibit here? What negative qualities?

2. If this is the protagonist, how, specifically, can he be made more admirable? How, specifically, can this protagonist be made more heroic? How, specifically, can this protagonist be made more sympathetic?

3. If this is the secondary protagonist, what do we learn about her? How, specifically, could this characterization be strengthened or deepened?

Companions You Can Count On   91

4. If this is the antagonist, how specifically can he be made more believable? How, specifically, can his villainy be disguised in the story?

5. How, specifically, does the writer express feelings in this scene/ segment? Does the writer engage *your* feelings as listener? If so, how, specifically, does the writer accomplish that? How, specifically, might the writer have done so more effectively?

6. What was the *hook*, the emotion or action that gives the scene impact? How, specifically, could that hook be made stronger, more intense?

7. Are there any specific aspects of writing style that you found intrusive? Are there any specific aspects of writing style you found in need of polish?

8. What, specifically, is the single thing you liked best about this scene/segment? Liked least?

When the reading is finished, give your listener(s) adequate time to complete their notes on the above questions. Then, ask them for verbal commentary. Listen attentively and take notes. Do not comment. Whatever is said, do not disagree or explain or defend your work. Thank your listener(s) for the generous input. Ask each listener if you may keep the notes that person has made. Thank your listener(s) yet again.

Give yourself a reasonable period of time to regain whatever emotional distance this critique process may have jeopardized. Re-read your listener's notes and your notes from the commentary sessions. Think and *feel* which comments and suggestions would be good for your work, make it stronger, give it more impact, make it more attractive to an editor. Edit your work accordingly.

Are You There Yet?

A HANDS-ON EXERCISE

I speak frequently in this book about your writer's journal. Let me explain what it is and what it is not. It is not your personal journal, the written record of your ruminations about your personal life. The writer's journal is a record of and workbook for your writing life. It is your repository for bits of experience, observation, and thought destined for eventual use in one writing project or another. The entries in a personal journal tend to be abstract, but the entries in a writer's journal should be concrete.

What you include in your writer's journal depends on the type of writing you do. If you are writing fiction, your writer's journal should include anything and everything that could be used in story-telling, especially for creating scenes: snatches of dialogue, either overheard or imagined; setting details, employing all of your senses; scenes or segments of scenes, each with conflict at its center; character descriptions, from real life or imagination; possible conflicted character interactions, including any of the above that could apply to that interaction.

The writer's journal allows you to access your life as material for your work. Life is a growth process for you, your stories, and your characters. You must make maximum use of your day-to-day life as a source of vitality for your fiction. Everything that happens to you, and to everyone around you, is grist for your storytelling mill. Here are some specific suggestions to set that mill grinding toward optimum output.

THE WRITER'S JOURNAL—HOW TO GO ABOUT IT

I. Choose a special notebook to be your writer's journal. Go on a

serious quest to find the perfect vehicle, the notebook that resonates for you in that visceral, even mystical way writing materials—
notebooks, pens, black lead pencils for Stephen King—have a way
of resonating for a writer.

Possible sources include notebooks you already own, a book
you could make yourself, stationery shops, office supply stores,
and college bookstores (my personal favorite).

II. Set aside journaling time at the end of each day. Begin that time
by thinking about what happened to you that day, reflecting on
unpleasant experiences as well as pleasant ones. Think specifically
about the following, and record in your journal as you think:

1. The new people you've seen or met—what you learned from
    and about them, what you might imagine about them.

2. New ways of thinking about or looking at concrete things (peo-
    ple, events, specific circumstances) that might have come to
    you that day. If you anticipate writing in this vein at the end
    of each day, you will find such fresh notions occurring to you
    more regularly than ever before.

3. Anything that may have happened to you that could be a learn-
    ing opportunity for you and for your story. Record what you
    learned. Even small events can teach something new.

    Make specific notes on how these encounters, observa-
    tions, and opportunities can be written into the lives of the
    characters in your story. Or, note how these encounters, obser-
    vations, and opportunities reveal lessons your characters have
    yet to learn.

    The most significant result of this exercise will be your
    heightened awareness of all that happens to you each day, as
    well as a new appreciation for the vast resource your day-to-
    day life can be for your work.

III. Set aside a separate section of your writer's journal. Title that section, "An Emotional Diary." In this section, record:

   1.   The emotions you experienced that day, with notes on their circumstances. Don't go on and on. Be succinct and keep to the point. Use precise images.

   2.   Engage the senses in each of these entries. What was going on for you sensually as you experienced each of these emotions? What were you seeing, hearing, smelling, tasting, touching at the time? Be very specific. Try to use unique metaphors to describe these sensations.

       Make note of how you might transport these emotions and sensations into the situations and experiences of your characters.

IV. An exercise for employing the above:

   1.   Write a scene about something that happened to you that day.

   2.   First, write that scene from your usual writer's journal point of view, most likely in the first person.

   3.   Then, rewrite that scene from another point of view. You could try using third person, with yourself as narrator, or the point of view of another person in the scene.

       Compare and contrast the entries. Also compare and contrast the experience (your feelings) you had while writing each of these entries.

Passage 5

WELL BEGUN GETS IT DONE

"Well begun is half done" is another saying that reminds me of my grandmother—and of the writing craft. I wouldn't go so far as to say that a strong story opening is half the battle of writing a novel, but it certainly is a major victory. As I have mentioned before, one of the most frequent faults of manuscripts submitted to editors is that those manuscripts are dull. They fail to stir up excitement in the reader, and excitement is what editors want in a story—right from the start.

Unless you are fairly advanced in your career—meaning, unless you are already successfully published—your submission feeds into a crowded system along with hundreds of others. Even if your submission package is addressed to a senior editor, it's not likely to be read by her. Your manuscript will be passed on to an editorial assistant, who will be the first reader of your work. Unfortunately, most of the proposals he reads are dull enough to put a caged tiger to sleep. I know this because I've been there.

Your challenge, as a writer, is to submit a story so intense and riveting it will catapult that young editor out of his ennui straight into grateful fandom for your work. In order to do this, you must grip his attention from your very first line. Fail to do so, and his interest lags with each sentence until he's back in lethargy-land yet again and your manuscript is on the return-to-sender pile.

Secret #21: Blood on the Floor

You must open your story where the excitement begins or, as we say in the mystery/suspense genre, when the blood is on the floor. Forget about those nineteenth-century Gothic novels that open up with long, brooding descriptions of the weather or with enough recounting of the characters' genealogy to make your eyes cross. Avoid opening with pages of sumptuous detail establishing the social status of the characters. The trick to hooking an editor with your opening is to begin your story in the middle of things. Specifically, start where the tension or conflict is first introduced into the life of your protagonist—and not a paragraph before.

Speaking of blood on the floor, what do you think about a murder mystery where the initial killing doesn't happen till page 158? I received such a manuscript, and it portrayed some wonderful characters and even some signs of tension between them. But, though the opening scene had some action in it, it wasn't enough to drag us fully and irrevocably into the story, as should be the case. If that case had been penned by Agatha Christie in that bygone golden age of mystery writing, she might have gotten away with a slow start. (Although a 158-page intro is pushing the envelope even for Agatha and her generation of mystery authors.)

This manuscript came to me much more recently than the Agatha Christie era. My editorial verdict had to be that, in order to create the kind of high stakes tension readers of this genre currently demand, the murder needed to happen about a hundred and fifty pages sooner than it did. Unfortunately, the story was built around an elaborate insurance scam. Because of the way the author structured the story, setup of the scam was necessary to give the murder context and to rouse interest in the victim. Without that background, the reader most likely wouldn't give a hoot whether he'd been knocked off or not. I tried to come up with alternate plotting scenarios, but each of those would have required a near total revamping of the story. As an editor, I'm perfectly comfortable with proposing extensive revisions, but I draw the line at what amounts to rewriting the story. This manuscript was rejected and returned to the author without a request to see it again.

Another submission I received was only marginally better. This author took one hundred and twenty-five pages to set up his story. The author dramatizes a long opening scene where a sexy woman shows up, and the protagonist, Angelo, trails after her like a hound on the scent. There is amusement value in this scene, but the sexy lady is a construct rather than a person who comes to life on the page. She is a device whose only purpose in the book is to illustrate something about the main character. Plus, that main character's behavior in this scene damages our respect for him and jeopardizes our motivation to care deeply about what happens to him.

This author's characterization choices may be cute at first, even engaging, but only temporarily so. Inevitably, they grow irritating, primarily because of the degree to which they slow our plunge into the main conflict of the story. They delay and distract us from arriving at the excitement of the story situation soon enough to inspire any real attachment to the characters and what will happen to them.

I did make some revision suggestions for this one. I recommended junking the sexy lady interchange altogether in favor of starting out with a scene that is more integral to the story. This would involve nixing approximately the first hundred pages of the manuscript. I advised that the author skip ahead to a scene where the story actually begins to show us what is happening to Angelo, rather than telling us about it. The revised opening scene also would have to do so in a context that draws us to him as a character. This suggestion would require, in my estimation, a story revision rather than a rewrite. I did, in this case, request to see the next incarnation of Angelo's story.

Renowned editor Michael Korda once remarked that two of the most difficult decisions for a novelist involve where to start a story and where to end it. When grappling with the former of those decisions, look for that puddle on the floor and the intense, dramatic, compelling situation that put it there. And if you want to make your exciting opening work for an editor—and for a reader—create that puddle of conflict at the expense of your protagonist every time.

Secret #22: Hot Water From the Start

In the most dramatic openings, the conflicted situation that starts the story already exists prior to page one. The inciting incident sets up the problem that will create trouble and conflict for the protagonist. A change—the more drastic, the better—has occurred. The story begins in the middle of things, as that change is happening or just after it has happened. This change propels the story, and the protagonist, into action. All of this constitutes the narrative hook. Your protagonist is thrust into difficulty right away. The reader, in turn, is thrust into your story via an intense, exciting opening.

The inciting incident must be an event powerful enough to trigger a chain of further events. In other words, the inciting incident must trigger action. This incident should be surprising, to protagonist and reader alike, and should happen as close to page one as possible.

This incident confronts your protagonist with a circumstance that will change his life in a substantial way, maybe forever. This circumstance need not be life-threatening, though an element of fear and dread definitely should be involved. This circumstance could range from a sense of something familiar slipping away to the actual onset of peril and danger, preferably in a world that was previously safe and secure, or at least appeared to be. Either way, something very important is at stake.

In some respect, this disrupting situation poses a direct threat to your protagonist's goals and desires—what he wants and needs for himself or for someone else. He must make a conscious decision to act in response to this situation and this threat. If he doesn't act, dire consequences will come to pass. He must do something and do it *now*. This initial action, or decision to act, sets the story in motion.

Obstacles are already evident in the circumstances your protagonist is being forced into. You can add even greater intensity to your opening, and to your story, by placing additional obstacles in your protagonist's path. As romantic suspense author Adrianne Lee says, "Give your hero or heroine lots of problems." Each of these problems should be in direct opposition to your protagonist's goals. She is propelled onward by conflict right from the outset of your story.

The genre or category in which you are writing will determine, in part, the nature of what is at stake and the specifics of the inciting incident. In romance novels and much of women's fiction, the story begins with a heroine about to be plunged into a situation that will change her life, usually because of a dramatic event in her romantic life. In mystery and suspense fiction, the stakes are even higher, dealing with matters of life and death. In science fiction and adventure books, elements of a malevolent unknown combine with projected dangers threatening to overwhelm the protagonist, often in an alternative universe. In adventure stories, inciting incidents arise within the context of perilous or hostile environments and are exacerbated by those environments.

Whatever the genre, the protagonist generally makes his decision to take action in response to the dilemma at hand near the end of the opening scene. Subsequent scenes find him undertaking this initial action, meeting with less than success, and barely escaping the dire consequences he dreads. These narrow escapes up the ante for him and deepen his commitment while intensifying his dread. The conflict, both internal and external, escalates. He will struggle in the context of these conflicts for the remainder of the book. You have dropped your protagonist into hot water at the beginning of your story. Your storytelling task is to raise the temperature of that water steadily higher until the incendiary climax at the end.

Of course, this must be happening to a character we care about. Otherwise, you risk the Rhett Butler reaction: "Frankly, author, I don't give a damn." Unfortunately, in yet another ill-fated arrival at my editorial desk, it was difficult at best to give a damn about the unworthy protagonist Jesse.

Straight from page one, Jesse came across as more nonplussed than clever. Her circumstances were decidedly precarious, creating lots of high stakes tension in her story situation. But I didn't, for a moment, believe that Jesse was equal to the challenges facing her. Because of the way she was portrayed, I found myself exasperated by her crippling consternation rather than empathetic toward it. Instead of acting or even thinking about acting, she stood there like a deer in the headlights until someone else appeared on the scene to act on her behalf.

Jesse's passivity may be human and understandable, but it doesn't make for a protagonist we care enough about to follow throughout an entire book. She does pull herself together and become more of an active principal later in the story, but it doesn't happen soon enough. By the time she becomes a more developed character, her author has missed the opportunity to make the strong first impression that would have tied a reader's hopes to Jesse from the start.

One way to plunge your empathetic hero into deep, hot water is with a prologue—a scene enacting an event from the past that fulfills the requirements of a dramatic opening. This event must be highly active, gripping, and fraught with conflict. It must change your character's life. A well-written prologue could have solved the problems with the opening of, Danny's story, yet another submission I received.

That opening was lackluster and overly expository, with nothing that excited my interest. The story was supposed to be a suspense thriller, but I found no evidence of that in its beginning pages. The author failed to explode into the story. He didn't open where the excitement of the story began. A prologue could have done just that by dramatizing an intense and riveting scene from the past instead of squandering the potential for opening impact in background exposition. Rather than being told *about* the terrible thing that happened in Danny's past, the reader wants to see it acted out. If there is strong dramatic action in the past of your protagonist, if the consequences of that action resonate in your story, or if those consequences are causing your present story to happen, consider dramatizing that pivotal past event in a prologue. Make that prologue powerful, startling, and short.

Set your prologue in the moment when the action is happening; never present it as a flashback. Maybe there are story circumstances where a flashback opening could work, but that is hardly ever the case because the impact of immediacy is lost. The reader is too aware of being carried back into the past, and is at least once removed from the experience of being catapulted into present difficulties along with the character.

Flashbacks in general are a source of editorial irritation for many readers and editors. By flashback, I'm referring to a full-fledged scene, usually spanning one to three pages, in which the action moves out of the space and time of the present into another space and time. This other time is usually the past, though thinking ahead to what will or may be coming—a flash forward—follows the same principle and annoys just as much.

By flashback, I don't mean the occasional instance of a character thinking of times gone by. Such thoughts can provide important background information, as long as they involve only a sentence or two, a paragraph at most. Nonetheless, I advise caution in these instances, also. Even these mini-breaks in chronological time sequence can disrupt the all-important forward momentum of your story.

In order for a flashback to work, the reader must be deeply immersed in the present story. That reader must be so inextricably hooked that she won't mind you yanking her out of that engrossing story present for a few pages to learn about the character's past, especially if that past is shaping the character's present. For this reason, a flashback is a dicey device to try in your opening pages, before the story has gained the momentum it needs to rivet reader attention. A prologue is almost always the way to go at this point in your story under these circumstances, because it can plunge your character into hot water from the start.

Secret #23: The Hook Line That Sinks 'Em

Your goal is to write a perfectly crafted opening sentence for your novel. Perfectly crafted to be what, you ask? This all-important sentence must, first of all, be attention-getting. Think of the last time you were in a bookstore. Picture the customers in the aisles, picking up books at random, or even purposefully. What do most of them do once they have that book in their hands? They may start by reading the back blurb, if the book is a paperback, or the flap copy, if it's a hardcover. In your own novels, you have no control of cover content. You do have control over the experience of what the bookstore browser does next, because most often his next move is to open the book to the first page and read, beginning with the opening line.

Here is your opportunity to hook the reader from the get-go. Your task is to craft an opening sentence that will pull the bookstore browsing reader into your story. This sentence should be straightforward, no convolutions or extraneous phrases allowed. You are aiming for hearts and minds here. A straight-shot, declarative, brief, and punchy sentence is your best bet for hitting both of those targets dead-on. Your goal is to startle in some way, to rouse curiosity about what your story will be. You do that with an opening sentence that is, most significantly of all, emotionally charged.

So, here's the exercise. Think about the beginning of your story. Take notes in response to the following:

1. What exactly is the nature of the moment in your protagonist's life when the story opens? What, specifically, makes this a moment of high interest in your story?
2. Your protagonist is, at this moment, being plunged into a situation where she will feel as if the world is being yanked out from under her. Why, specifically, does your protagonist have this feeling?
3. From this point on, the world of your protagonist and this story will never be the same again. How, specifically, will that world be changed?

4. From this moment on, your protagonist will be engaged in *struggle*.
    Where, in general, will that struggle lead?

Reread the notes you have taken in response to these questions. Put
the paper aside. Next, do the following:

1. Close your eyes. Put your head on your desk or table.
2. Focus inward. Take some deep breaths to help you achieve that.
3. Visualize your story opener happening. Imagine your opening
    scene actually taking place.
4. Use your senses—all of them. Imagine the sounds of your opening
    scene, then the smells, the tactile sensation of the air on skin, the
    taste of emotion in the mouth of your character.
5. Invite a sentence to begin forming in your mind. Focus on making
    this a dramatic sentence, a sentence that introduces your story in
    a powerful way.
6. Write this sentence down, along with any others that arise. Do
    this with your eyes still closed or only halfway open.

Open your eyes all the way. Reread what you've written. Work on
it. Craft it. Hone it down. Create a first sentence that is:

• Concise—economy of words, declarative style.
• Intriguing—a hook to make readers wonder right away what's
  going on here.
• Surprising—to grab the reader's attention.
• Emotional—takes us into the *feelings* of the character at this
  opening moment.
• Memorable—because it is all of the above.

Sometimes a line like this will just come to you, like a gift from heaven. You'll be walking along or driving your car or taking laundry out of the dryer and there it is—the perfect opening line, fully formed and miraculous in your mind. When such a gift comes, you must be absolutely certain not to squander it. Don't trust your memory. You'll feel confident that you could never forget such a perfect sentence. Take my word for this: You can forget it, and you very likely will.

When heaven sends you a gift, honor it. Whatever you are doing when that happens, stop in your tracks. Pull your car to the side of the road. Leave the laundry where it falls. Grab a notebook, the one you always must have with you. Write that sentence down. You've been mightily blessed.

Davidson's story could have used such a blessing. I won't quote the first line here in respect for maintaining the author's anonymity. This was a story set in the present, but the opening line had to do with political events of the 1970s. This might have been okay if the story began with a past prologue, but it didn't. The sentence was also long, rambling, and unexceptional. It provided information, but delivered no surprise. The author's otherwise fine writing style was not apparent in his opening line.

Almost as unfortunate as the first line's lack of impact on the reader was the way it misled the reader. This first line had to do with the president of the United States and his connection with the previously mentioned past events. Placing this information in the prominent first sentence position leads us to believe this is the subject of the story. Yet, neither the president nor this long-gone political period figures with much significance in the novel. As the editor reading this proposal, I was stymied when it came to understanding why the author would have chosen such an opener. He had squandered the opportunity to make a powerful first impression.

This author began with background. He failed to take into account the browsing shopper standing in the bookstore aisle reading first pages, hoping to be set afire by what he finds there. He also forgot about me, the editor, wading through stacks of manuscripts, longing to discover a spark of brilliance among them.

You must understand that making an impressive first impression is not to be confused with pretentiousness. The first line of Hudson's story wasn't even written by him. Hudson's story opens up with a quote—a rather long one—followed by a long chapter title. Both of these distract us, as readers, from the story to come, rather than pulling us into it. In fact, since both the quote and the chapter title are couched in lofty, pseudo-Victorian diction in what is supposed to be a suspense novel, this opening could turn off potential readers of that genre altogether.

Sometimes, authors try to wow readers and editors with displays of verbal erudition. These authors believe they will prove how clever and literary they are by salting their writing with complicated sentences and high-flown language. The object of all writing is to communicate, and to do so clearly. The object of fiction writing is to tell a story that will involve the reader emotionally, which is not at all the same thing as engaging the reader intellectually. Verbal pyrotechnics, however educated they may sound, interfere with the reader's ability to connect with the story, which is the last thing a novelist should do—especially in the opening line.

Writing the opening line of a novel is a big responsibility for an author. It deserves serious thought, planning, and attention to craft. The opening line must plant a narrative hook in the reader's psyche so deep there'll be no letting go until the dramatic end of the very taut storyline attached to that hook. Never underestimate the potential power of your opening line to hook your reader from the start.

Polish this line into a real jewel that will dazzle your reader and set him wondering what will happen next.

Here are some options for the form of your concise, surprising, riveting, memorable opening sentence:

- A startling exclamation in dialogue.
- An intriguing statement.
- A comment on something or someone strange.
- A comment about an unusual aspect of setting.
- A brief statement alluding to a disaster or pending disaster.

These are only a few of the many options you might use. Your choice of which option works for your story has a lot to do with the mood and tone of that story. If you are writing a suspense novel, choose an opening that evokes a suspenseful tone—an atmosphere of mystery and apprehension with a suggestion of something ominous lurking very close at hand. Thus, you pull the reader instantly and effectively into the world of your story by establishing the mood of that world and making the reader feel it from the start.

Continue to enhance this mood throughout the first paragraph and the remainder of the first page by including precise details that appeal to the senses. Use these sparingly. The perfect single detail that resonates with the mood and emotion of the scene is far more effective than a laundry list of observations that buries the reader in too much too soon. Less is more here, as long as that less is the best.

Be sure that the tone you establish in the first line and the ensuing paragraph is consistent with the tone of the rest of the book. If you're writing a comedy or light romance, don't open in a brooding tone. Don't try to catch the reader off guard with clever misdirection of mood. You will only confuse, maybe even irritate, your audience.

You want to transport your reader to the appropriate emotional territory for experiencing your story from the start.

One aspiring author whose manuscript went straight to my second read pile (and that's a good thing) was creating a suspense story—a heartrending tale of a child in jeopardy. The author began the opening paragraph with what might have been an idyllic image of that child swinging in a playground. But even in the supposedly carefree first line, the swing chain squeaks and grinds abrasively with each back and forth movement. Then, the child falls. The author has set us up to be startled, and we are. She foreshadows ominous events, the fall of our hopes for this child, which are to come. She hooked me from the opening line, and that made all the difference.

Let's end this section with a small exercise. Go to your bookshelves. Take down several novels at random from different genres and varying levels of artistry. It doesn't matter if you've read them or not. Open each book to the first page, and write down the first line of the story, allotting each line a separate page of your writer's journal. Under each of these first lines, write the answers to the following questions:

1. Does this sentence give you the sense of being at the middle of things with something exciting about to happen? If so, how does it accomplish that?
2. Is this line concise and straightforward, rather than rambling?
3. Is this line rhythmic? Catchy? Does it have a ring to it?
4. Is this line intriguing or startling? If so, how?
5. Does this line make you wonder what happens next?
6. Could this line use more work, more careful crafting? If so, rewrite it effectively so that your revised hook sentence will evoke a positive answer to all of the above.

Secret #24: Beware of Beleaguered Backstory

Too many new writers begin their stories by filling us in on character history. For instance, the saga of Jack and Jim is a buddy story about two quirky characters. The author apparently doesn't trust us to pick up on just how quirky they are from merely reading about their present behavior, so she tells us *a lot* about their background histories, both separately and together. She does this at the beginning of the story as she introduces them. She could have immersed us in the present story by showing us Jack and Jim in action and dialogue, dramatizing their personalities in a concrete way. Instead, she tells us who they are in narrative. More specifically, she tells us who they were long before the story began.

She does spotlight a particular scene from the past, though she doesn't permit the characters to act it out. The scene is funny, but not pivotal or riveting enough to justify being written into a prologue. Also, the subject of the scene has absolutely nothing to do with anything that happens in the book. Not only are we diverted from the story even before we've begun to know what the plot is, we're also sent the wrong signal regarding what the story will be about.

I suspect that the author was hoping to capture reader attention—that ubiquitous bookstore browser—with an amusing anecdote on page one. She actually did accomplish that with me. But my anticipation turned out to be short-lived, as was my enthusiasm for the manuscript once I realized I'd been misled. The Jack and Jim anecdote doesn't work as a story opener on many levels. For the purposes of this section, I focus on this submission as an example of beleaguering backstory, especially in the crucial first impression position. Another author might have a less calculating reason than this one for plunging us into backstory before hooking us on front story. Often, that reasoning has to do with the compulsion to tell all. You may be tempted to tell too much backstory in your own work. Your motives may even be magnanimous. You're convinced the reader needs to know this information in order to understand what's going on. But is that really true? How much of what you're telling us about the past does the reader absolutely have to know to comprehend the single event that is happening right now at this opening moment of the present story?

Reread that last question slowly several times. Copy it into your writer's journal. Imprint it on your psyche forever, because this is the question you must answer every time you feel compelled to leave the ongoing flow of your story and digress backward in time to fill us in. Rule of thumb: Include only the bare minimum of background detail necessary to keep the average, intelligent reader from being confused. All else may be preparation for story or rumination on story or noodling toward story, but it isn't story itself.

Don't tell me you're using backstory to establish character, either. I've heard that one way too many times. Your job isn't to establish character or anticipate character or politely introduce us to character. Your job is to plop that character abruptly down in front of us, to shove us into his life at a point where that life is already slipping into conflict and crisis. He's in hot water, and we're dumped in there with him. Never dilute the impact of that because you can't resist the urge to interject a tidbit from character history, however yummy that tidbit may be. Keep us up to our necks in a story so fascinating we can't think of anything but what is happening right now and what could possibly happen next.

So, what do you do with all the wonderful material you've generated from the "Writing Characters From the Inside Out" exercise and other fruitful sources? First of all, you use that material to inform the story—and yourself—as you write. You will most likely not include much of this background material in the novel itself. However, it will be obvious from the way you write the story—your deep knowledge of and sensitivity toward your characters, in particular—that you are the godlike, all-knowing creator of that story and the reader can trust your telling of it.

Inevitably, some of that background material will appear on the page. But always keep this rule of thumb in mind: Only include background details that are absolutely necessary for the reader to understand the current action at whatever point that action may be. I think of this technique of incorporating backstory as doling out crumbs to birds, just enough to keep them hopping along the path behind you and in step with your story, not a morsel more.

In the opening pages, you must be even more sparing. Here, there can be almost no justification for distracting us from the forward movement of your story erupting into life. Here, you must keep us constantly on point, on the scene and in it with your characters. What happens to them is happening to us. This is where the author's natural compulsion to tell all is at its most compelling. You must resist. The successful birth of your story depends on it.

Secret #25: Putting You in the Picture From Page One

I've already mentioned that two of the hardest decisions for a novelist are where to begin a story and where to end it. What about when to start writing? Here's an approach to that which involves building suspense—not in the story, but in yourself.

Get the planning stuff out of the way. Work on the "Writing Characters From the Inside Out" exercises for your big three characters. Add to that the information generated from practicing other exercises in this book, also meant to help you get to know the people of your story and what happens to them. Record all of the above by whatever system works for you. Do all of this head stuff for as long as you can stand it without writing a word of text.

Hold yourself back from the writing until you're not just ready to write, but dying to write. At that near-desperate point, the writer in you will be closest emotionally to the intensity your story needs. Use that intensity, that frustration, that explosive creative energy, to conjure within yourself the dramatic state that will feed the true life, soul, and emotions of your characters and their situations. Focus the power of all of that inward into your story, then outward toward the page. Now, face that page and *write*.

Think of the writing of your opening scene as the beginning of a hands-on quest to discover what kind of novel you want this to be. Your goal is to be able to define, by the end of this first scene, just what you are going for here, at least in this opening, if not yet in the story as a whole. Figure out what this opening needs to get your characters and their story across to the reader. Visualize the first impression you want the reader to have of what your story is really about. If you know what that impression should be, you are far more likely to achieve it on the page. When you have determined what your aim is, the style of your storytelling will adjust itself accordingly.

The specific process by which you begin will be different each time with each story. That is as it should be. Otherwise, you can go stale and start pumping out types of stories rather than stories themselves. Worse yet, you will rob yourself of the true joy of the process, the joy of discovery. It is important and affirming to let yourself experience that discovery anew every time you start a book, to seek and find the appropriate process for writing one story, then the next. This is key among the adventures, the surprises, the revelations of writing that keep it always fresh, never hackneyed, at least not for you as author.

Expect that these epiphanies—what the book is, how to go about writing it—will happen for you a little at a time. Don't expect a full-blown shocker of a vision, though once in a great blessed while the universe gifts you with one of those. In the meantime, don't fret. Let it all evolve at its own pace. Don't hamstring your imagination by insisting you have to do a certain thing a certain way. Do it whatever way comes most naturally at the moment. Trust your writer's instinct to guide you toward that natural mode. Most of all, trust that such an instinct resides in you. If you don't believe that now, just take my word for it. The secret is to let go of your will, at least for the time being, and go along with whatever happens after that.

Nonetheless, be aware that the style of the opening should set up what is to come. For example, Ella is the amateur sleuth protagonist of a manuscript proposal for a mystery novel. Mystery novels and their protagonists are motivated by the quest for truth. This quest, this mission—to excavate authenticity from a pit of lies, secrets, and misdirections—should begin with commitment and continue apace. There must be a dogged relentlessness about it.

In Ella's story, a body is found, and the pace lopes on. From the beginning, the writing and the style of storytelling are smooth and rhythmic and mesmerizing—no doggedness, no relentlessness, no urgency. That style doesn't work for the mystery genre. The author, and Ella, should have noodled around a while longer. The author should have written *at* the story—throwing out words, making sentences, attacking the story idea. She should have let all of that pour forth until the style felt right for the story. She should have listened for her writer's instinct to guide her toward that rightness. The author stopped too soon in what should have been her own quest—to discover what the story needed to be and how that need dictated the manner in which it must be written.

Trusting that you are capable of coming to such a discovery is like saying, "I'll know it when I see it." Except that, in this case, the operative phrase is, "I'll know it when I feel it." When that happens, you will feel it as only you can. I regret that, on the subject of style and substance and putting those together at the start, I can't get much clearer than I am here. After all, we're talking about instinct. A lot of that discussion is beyond words, or maybe behind them. So don't fret if some of this sounds vague to you. Simply tuck it into the back of your mind and semi-forget about it till the epiphanies come. And they will come. Trust me on that.

Crossroads

AN AUTHOR SELF-INTERROGATION

After you have written your story opening, take a day off to let it settle on the page and in your mind. Then, ask it the following questions and record the answers in your writer's journal. Some of these interrogations will sound familiar to you. We have previously addressed similar storytelling issues. Now, we encounter these questions yet again, this time in reference to your opening scene as a whole. They continue to apply.

1. What is dramatic about the scene? Be specific. Answer from gut level, where dramatic impact is most surely felt.
2. What does this opening line sound like when I read it to myself? Is there a rhythm to it? Is it the rhythm I want for this story?

3. What is going on at the moment this story opens? Are we in the middle of something?

4. What is happening to my character in this first scene? Is it something extraordinary? Is this a situation that will change this character's life? Does the character sense this change happening? Will the reader sense it as well and feel compelled to read on?

5. What does this character look like? Is this description rendered via a couple of significant details, rather than by interrupting the forward action of the scene to describe appearance at length?

6. Does this scene establish that something significant is at stake for this character, and perhaps for others as well? Will dire circumstances ensue if this character fails to succeed?

7. Are obstacles to that success already evident, or at least hinted at, in this scene?

8. Does this character make a conscious decision to act in response to the situation introduced in this scene? Does this decision set the story in motion?

9. Is this character a person with whom the reader will wish to identify?

10. Is this character motivated to act by something the reader can relate to and find sympathetic?

11. Does the action of the story begin immediately, preferably within the first few sentences of the scene?

12. Is there at least a line or two of dialogue on the first page?

13. Is the tone or mood of the story established accurately in this scene? Does this tone evoke an atmosphere that pulls the reader instantly and convincingly into the world of the story?

14. Does this scene create a strong sense of reality? Do specific details that lend authenticity to the scene, making the setting recognizable and/or believable?

15. Are time and place apparent, though not dwelt upon, in this scene?
16. Does this scene avoid long passages of background exposition?
17. Does the action of this scene move chronologically forward, avoiding flashbacks and flash-forwards?
18. Does the scene create tension by having the character failing to triumph over the obstacles presented and barely escaping the consequences of that failure?

Are You There Yet?

A HANDS-ON EXERCISE

Some of you have already written your opening scene; some of you have not. For the former, this exercise will involve rewriting the scene; for the latter, this exercise will involve writing the scene for the first time. Whichever the case may be, I urge you to do the following:

1. Skim through this passage on dramatic openings. Don't read in-depth or try to memorize. Simply remind yourself of what is here.
2. Fold your hands on your desk, put your head down on top of them, close your eyes, and focus in on the ideas that stand out most vividly to you from skimming the passage. Sit quietly with these ideas for a few moments, breathing deeply into them.
3. Open your eyes, lift your head, and begin to freewrite a dramatic opening for your story, whether for the first or the fortieth time.

Passage

DOES THIS SCENE GO THE DISTANCE?

The dramatic intensity imperative applies as much to individual scenes as it does to novels as a whole. The reader must be drawn into each scene and held fast by what is happening there. Some scenes won't be as emotionally charged as others. A super-charged scene is what we call a big scene—a scene that not only propels the story forward, as every scene must do, but catapults the story a quantum leap ahead. Such a scene surprises us in a substantive way. We learn something new or shocking that hooks us more deeply into the story. Big scenes are major storytelling opportunities, as well as major storytelling challenges.

Secret #26: Set Your Course Toward Drama

Imagine that we, as readers, are in a black stretch funeral limousine. Grief and tension crowd the space behind dark-tinted windows and a slide that shuts the driver out of hearing. Death resolved nothing. It has created new ambiguities, lacerated old wounds. We're grave-yard-bound in the first car behind the hearse. The dialogue around us is taut and revealing. The characters riding with us are insightfully described. We're right here in this fraught moment as the cemetery gates approach. Line break. Next paragraph: We're back in the limo headed away from the cemetery.

We stare at the page. What happened? We anticipated a super scene at the gravesite: a confrontation, or police detectives wandering among the mourners, or a stranger lurking at the edge of the crowd. Instead, we're back in the car. More accurately, we're no longer anywhere in this story at all. We've been wrenched out of the life of the scene and snapped back to reality from our state of suspended disbelief. Omission of the graveside scene has interrupted the flow of action for us as readers. The author who submitted this manuscript squandered the dramatic potential of the scene and short-circuited reader involvement in her story, as well.

She also squandered this submission opportunity. As an editor of popular fiction, I look for exciting stories you stay up half the night reading because you can't stop turning pages. Commercial fiction is meant to sell in considerable numbers. Safely written, quiet stories don't often do that. Readers want to be swept up and carried along in a torrent of events happening to fascinating characters whose futures are in doubt. Win or lose, which will it be? The reader keeps turning pages to discover the answer. Only a truly dramatic tale can maintain reader commitment, from beginning to end.

This author suffers from a malady that afflicts many writers. She's too reserved and polite. She is also too self-protective. Intense subject matter is unsettling, upsetting, and even frightening or infuriating. Emotionally charged scenes can be uncomfortable to write. However, as a writer, you must concern yourself with pay dirt. These unsettling scenes, strategically spaced throughout the story, make a novel a page-turner. They carry the reader to dark places in the soul and also into the heart of strong storytelling. Will the main characters be extricated from this darkness? That is the central question of the story. An author can't hope to ask this question, much less answer it, without traversing that darkness herself.

Imagine another scenario. We're reading a mystery manuscript. For many chapters, we've been following the private investigator hero in pursuit of a nasty character. PI has been frustrated at every turn, unable to get to his nemesis. PI loses his objectivity toward this particular villain, much as Sherlock Holmes does toward Moriarty in the famous Sir Arthur Conan Doyle series. We're poised for the confrontation we've been repeatedly promised is on the way. We flip pages in a flurry of expectation. Then, PI and perpetrator meet for the first time, and nothing happens. PI recognizes the villain, but doesn't confront him. Once again, we, the readers, are left staring at the page. We toss the book aside, or against a wall, as frustrated as our PI protagonist led us to believe he was.

If this frustration of reader expectations had been a deliberate building of our emotions toward a disastrous encounter later in the story, the device could have worked. No such apocalyptic confrontation between good and bad occurred anywhere in this novel. When I asked the author why not, he said, "I wanted to be unique." No matter how adamantly I attempted to convince him of the difference between originality and storyteller suicide, he refused to agree. He insisted on disappearing at disaster time. He should have dashed toward that disaster instead.

I'm assuming you've created the perfect protagonist for your story. The next thing you must do is thrust him into serious trouble, as close to the beginning of the story as possible. Something is happening to your protagonist that will change his life significantly, and not for the better. The world as he's known it is slipping away beneath his feet. Trouble arrives with its sidekicks, threat and danger. A lot is at stake for this character, and others as well. The stakes in this story situation, and in each scene, are a matter of life and death.

This threat of death—whether it means loss of physical, psychic, emotional, or spiritual life—intensifies the suspense that lurks at the heart of all compelling storytelling. This suspense keeps the reader wondering: "How can this character I've come to care about possibly extricate herself from this situation? How will this story turn out?"

These questions create a sense of urgency in the story. At least one of these elements—suspenseful questions, urgency, or threat of consequences—must be present in every scene of your story. Otherwise, the scene fails to enhance tension, and the storyline goes slack. One of two things must happen for your story to succeed: The scene must be reworked to perform its proper dramatic function, or it must be omitted altogether.

In fiction writing terms, very few problems are as drastic as neglecting to establish and maintain story conflict. Conflict arises as soon as your protagonist's goal is thwarted in some way. From that point on, he's in trouble. The more serious the trouble, the more intense the conflict, the more rapidly the pages turn. The secret of great storytelling is as simple as that. The conflict in your dramatic situation is only as strong as the trouble your character is struggling against, on some level, in every scene you write.

In popular or commercial fiction, this struggle is primarily external and physical. Some degree of physical action will be needed to resolve it. In literary fiction, the struggle is primarily internal and mental, brought on by the anguish of difficult choices, especially moral choices. In either case, your protagonist is on a collision course with disaster, and that is exactly where you want her to be.

Secret #27: Secrets, Lies, and Love

You've created a dramatic situation with the first of its essentials solidly engaged. Now, you must build the fires of that situation hot, hotter, hottest, little by little in every scene. You need story fuel—secrets and lies. Strong stories, whatever the category, are filled with secrets and lies. Protagonists lie and keep secrets for sympathetic reasons. Antagonists lie and keep secrets for unsympathetic reasons that right-thinking readers reject. The point is that everybody lies and keeps secrets, and a piece of those dramatic devices must be present in every scene.

This hidden reality—what is actually true for these characters, as opposed to what they lead us to believe is true—lurks beneath the surface of the scene. We as readers may not be aware of the existence of this truth. Some or most or maybe only one of the characters is out-of-the-know, as well. That alternate reality gradually may gather force to erupt from beneath the surface and give the story a substantial twist. Or, that reality may eke itself forth in bits and hints, making readers and characters alike more and more ill at ease, less and less trustful of our perceptions, until the light of truth finally dawns.

The former of these two storytelling choices, the eruption of previously hidden truth upon the scene, is more likely to occur in popular/commercial fiction. Characters and their situations are dramatically, perhaps even violently, disturbed, distressed, and disarranged by the revelation. The latter of these storytelling choices, the eking out of hints and bits, is more likely to occur in literary fiction. Characters and their situations are more subtly disturbed, distressed, and disarranged. The appropriate choice, the choice the author must make for each and every scene, is the one that works best for that scene in particular, as well as for that book as a whole. You must keep your protagonist on course toward inevitable disaster. You can't disappear at disaster time.

And don't forget the romance. An author friend from Queens, New York, pokes fun at both her borough and her chosen art by speaking of "the poipuses of the plot." Very little serves the "poipuses of a plot" better, when it comes to heightening story tension, than two people attempting against all odds to become a couple. There are countless ways to create and capitalize on these natural tensions. For example, you could apply the *Men are From Mars, Women are From Venus* principle to conflict-ridden romantic interactions.

Whatever the interpretation, or the orientation, two human beings in a love relationship provide endless possibilities for trouble, conflict, intensity, and drama. This potentially explosive interaction injects itself into the story at precisely the moment the protagonist least needs another complication. These two meet, and sparks fly. Those sparks are not all of the romantic/sexual variety. This pair is putty in service of the "poipuses of the plot." Remember what Mike Nichols says, "We only care about their humanity." However painstakingly we may have repressed the vulnerable, revealing aspects of ourselves, nothing forces that humanity more starkly to the surface than falling in love.

The greatest storytellers know this. Shakespeare knew it. Even tough guys like John le Carré and Tom Clancy know it. All good stories are about human interactions, especially the conflicted ones, and no interaction is more conflicted than a romantic relationship. Anyone who's ever been in love knows that. Anyone who's ever been in love, or who hopes to be in love or never to be in love again, is curious about this very problematic aspect of human experience. People are fascinated by the ways in which other human beings, including fictional ones, manage to traverse the romance minefield safely—or not.

It isn't just the sex in a romantic relationship that sells a story, though I'd be a prude and a prevaricator to deny that sex does sell. Look for more about writing that particular type of scene in passage seven of this book. Meanwhile, let's just say that very little suspension of disbelief is required for most readers to buy into the scenario of two romantically attracted people on a collision course with disaster.

Secret #28: Relationships Crave Conflict

Now that I've dragged us into the sticky pit of conflicted relationships, let's squirm ourselves truly stuck, then see what we might do to break free. Begin with this premise: If two people agree on everything, one of them is unnecessary. This may not be true in day-to-day life, unless you enjoy fireworks and frustration as a daily diet. However, this premise is absolutely true in fiction.

In my publishing house days, along with marshaling mystery novels into print, I also edited a line of Regency romance novels. This genre's roots were planted by Jane Austen in the nineteenth century and were nurtured by Georgette Heyer in the twentieth. The contemporary versions of these stories are often, though not exclusively drawing room comedies of manners, set in England during the Regency period of the early nineteenth century. While I was working in this genre, the following story proposal landed on my desk.

Phoebe has fallen on hard times, as is frequently the case with young Regency novel heroines. Her perfectly respectable country father has lost what money he had and has passed away, leaving Phoebe penniless and vulnerable—not good circumstances for a woman in most any era, especially the Regency. Being respectable, she has few options. One of those options is to become a governess, as did Charlotte Bronte's Jane Eyre. (Phoebe's story is a Regency romance rather than a Gothic one, so there's not likely to be a mad Mrs. Rochester salted away in the attic.)

Hapless Phoebe finds a governess position with an aristocratic family of distant relatives. She arrives early at the Mayfair, London, residence of her rich relative-employers. No one is there to greet her except Reginald, the decidedly inappropriate second son of Lord Darlington, fourth Earl of whatever. As second son, he has little chance of ascending to Daddy's earldom, so Reggie has become a something of a lovable scoundrel, a standard character type of Regency period novels.

So far, we are solidly in line with the conventions of the genre. Phoebe and Reginald banter back and forth. She is intelligent and articulate, though unfortunately plain-faced. He is cynical and drop-dead gorgeous. He secretly admires her wit. She secretly admires his well-turned calf. Scene one, in the foyer, a pattern commences— chance meeting, verbal skirmish, mild flirtation. Scene two, pattern repeats in the drawing room. Scene three, same old, in the garden. This story is putting me to sleep.

The life of a scene originates in the relationship between conflicting characters as they battle toe-to-toe on opposing sides of a crucial story situation. Phoebe and Reginald are never toe-to-toe in anything other than intellectual fashion. They get along too well for too long to create adequate story tension and intensity. Way before the third scene, true contention should be established between them.

I suggested that the author alter Phoebe's background somewhat. Perhaps her father lost his money and respectability because of a rake, or maybe her father was something of a rake himself. Either way, the family money was squandered, Phoebe was left penniless, and she is understandably at odds with Reggie's lifestyle. I have no idea whether or not the author chose either of these alternatives, because she didn't resubmit to me, though I requested she do so. I also never heard this author's name again. By the way, if an editor asks to see your work again, take him up on it. He's not just being nice. Editors aren't that nice.

You also must create believable interpersonal tension in scenes that have more than two opposing characters, though it's more difficult to do so. The more fine-tuned the tension focus, the greater the impact of the scene. How many characters are at odds in your scene? What are they at odds about? Answer these questions before writing.

Conflicted interactions may be portrayed between any two individuals in your cast of characters. The impact is greater when two of the big three characters are conflicting. These central characters—the protagonist, the protagonist's mate/sidekick/foil, and the antagonist—carry the major weight of the story. Whenever two of them are in a scene together with overt or even covert tension between them, that scene is important.

You must select actions, gestures, and dialogues that give the character interaction optimum impact for the reader. Casual interactions slow story momentum or, as with Phoebe and Reginald, fail to establish momentum. Take full advantage of dramatic potential. Make your character interactions demonstrate that something important is at stake right now for each of these characters.

Something important is also at stake for the relationship between these characters. The scene becomes an arena for playing out crucial issues. For the purposes of the plot, these areas of conflict will not be resolved until late in the story. They are exacerbated by what happens in earlier scenes. Whatever the outcome of a specific confrontation, by the end of the scene the situation of the characters and their relationship has changed. The agent of this change is character conflict.

The storytelling challenge is to imbed that conflict as subtext beneath the plot. I've adapted my "Writing Characters From the Inside Out" exercise for writing relationships from the inside out. This exercise will help you create that subtext and intensify character conflict as you reveal previously hidden depths—fears, desires, shameful secrets—in your characters. These revelations create subtext, the life of the scene lurking beneath its visible surface. Subtext erupts into text, and you have the trouble and conflict you need.

Before beginning this relationship exercise, develop each of your conflicting characters with the "Writing Characters From the Inside Out" exercise (if you haven't already). The discoveries you make from this preliminary work create a foundation for the discoveries you are about to make through the relationship exercise.

THE INSTRUCTIONS:

1. Write answers to the questions below in your writer's journal.
2. Write in the first person, using "I."
3. Write first as Character A (you are this character), answering all questions in reference to Character B.
4. Write next as Character B (you are this character), answering all questions in reference to Character A.
5. Follow the usual writer's journal guidelines for developing characters. (Concentrate on how the character *feels* about each question; answer from the *gut* of the character more than from the head; minimize rumination, theorizing, and abstractions and stick to the concrete; never be daunted by anything.)
6. If your knowledge of your story doesn't provide answers to these questions, expand that knowledge.

Substitute specific character names. If you haven't yet named your characters, do so now. A nameless character has less reality for you than a named character does.

THE QUESTIONS:

1. What is my major source of conflict with him?
2. What do I lead this person to believe I think about her?
3. What do I really think about him?
4. What do I say about this person behind her back?
5. What significant untruth have I told this person?
6. What significant secret have I kept from this person?
7. What past connections do this person and I have that have not yet been revealed?
8. What does this person think I want from him?
9. Add any other questions you would like to explore, and answer them.

Once you've completed this exercise, return to the scene you were writing. Place your characters in that scene, their selves and interactions newly informed by the exercise. If their previous interactions lacked spontaneity and surprise, if they were too predictable and unexciting, I guarantee that will no longer be the case.

Secret #29: Avoid Scenes We've Seen Too Often

In *The Art of Fiction*, John Gardner talks about the dream of the story, the absorbing world a writer must create in each book she writes. He wasn't referring to the dreams you have when you sleep, or to dream scenes as written in novels. At least, I hope he wasn't. I'd be relieved if I never had to read such a scene again. Many other agents and editors feel the same. Dream sequences are scene clichés, but they occur so often because writers like to write them. Since that's a tough current to paddle against, I'll accept the inevitable and simply offer some advice, beginning with an example.

In this scene, we understand from the start that we are someplace unusual. The character is flying, high enough to skim over everything, low enough for people on the ground to grab at her ankles and maybe even latch on. Each time that happens, she kicks free, but just barely. She must remain constantly vigilant or be dragged down, a possibility she deeply dreads, because those on the ground mean her nothing but harm.

This is a version of the common flying dream. This scene could work for a story in which the character's waking life is plagued by anxieties and adversaries. However, to hold reader attention, the flyer would have to touch down and also return to consciousness sooner than in this particular manuscript. The flight eventually ends, but the dream doesn't. The dream transports us to a barren landscape, where the character wanders, for quite some time, until we are transported to a stark white hallway with a line of closed doors on either side. The character walks to one of these doors, which happens to be painted black, and raises her fist to knock.

She's in that position when she hears a series of knocks and awakens. The knocks are from the non-dream world. Someone is at the door with news that moves the story forward. Thank heaven for that, because this dream has moved us nowhere—which is the problem with dream scenes in general. More often than not, they fail to do the work of a scene. They fail to advance the story. They also distract from the storyline.

The dream sequence described here goes on way too long. We're awakened from the flow of the story by wondering when this dream will end. If you insist upon including a dream scene in your novel, you must first find a way to make this scene enhance the plot, maybe by revealing significant information hidden in the character's subconscious. And you must keep it short. The same principles apply to scenes where the narrating character is drugged or experiencing any kind of abnormal psychic state.

Still, I haven't touched upon my strongest objections to these scenes: They are more often psychological manipulations than vehicles for seeking the emotional truth of the character and his situation. We are cued to believe that we're witnessing truth at a subconscious level. Most often, the story would be better served by a real-life dramatization of that truth in a scene. Concrete physical actions, reactions, dialogue, and narrative take us straight to the heart and soul of the character. No manipulations are needed.

Jessica Lange, a brilliant player of the emotional scene, has a strategy for reaching and expressing this emotional truth, as she explained in the television series "Inside the Actor's Studio." Her strategy applies to writing, as well as to performance. Her goal as actor, and yours as author, is to build a scene that is real rather than calculated. She warns against thinking about that goal up front.

If rage is the emotion you're striving for in a scene, don't begin by telling yourself, "I have to write rage now." Begin with the first and simplest emotion that is genuine for your character, and for you as writer, at the opening of the scene. Starting with that first real feeling and let one emotion follow another at its own natural pace. You're on the way to rage, but don't think about that. Simply let the scene build, one emotion to the next.

To do that, you must be *in* the scene, living it, feeling it. Place yourself mentally, psychically, and spiritually inside this single, precise moment. Surrender and submerge yourself in it. Tune in to each of your senses—sight, sound, touch, smell, taste—one at a time, then all together. Take note, in the deepest part of yourself, of everything that's going on. Be open to everything there is to feel at this point in the scene. One emotion becomes another and another, reaching a natural peak of intensity at the high point of the scene.

Secret #30: The Art of Milking the Scene

I often use films as examples of effective storytelling because more of us have seen the same movies than read the same books. This segment relies on the film *Places In the Heart* as an example of milking the scene for every last drop of drama. I begin, however, with a manuscript example from an author who was no milkmaid.

The protagonist was strong and engaging. The synopsis outlined a tale of emotional complexity and high stakes. The action kept me moving at a compelling pace, slow enough to allow for adequate development of characters and story lines, fast enough to keep the pages turning. I expected this skillfully controlled pacing to continue throughout the story. This was the first book in a proposed mystery series. The stakes for the protagonist were high. Life and death hung in the balance and could tip either way, the outcome to be decided in the final scene.

My rational editorial mind told me the protagonist was destined to survive. Otherwise, this would be a very short series. At the same time, my fully engaged reader mind was on tenterhooks, eager to know what was going to happen—and, how it would happen. I'd read nearly three hundred pages, captive to the narrative all the way. I'd come to care about this bemusing, humanly flawed character, now in great peril. I'd made a serious commitment to the story, and I was ready for the payoff.

Carried along by the momentum of the story. I spun into the

final scene, a high-action scene with a violent edge. I braced for that action. Then, all of a sudden, it was over. The scene had raced past me in a blur, at a pace something like: gallop, gallop, gallop, the end. I'd been dropped abruptly out of the story into the nonfiction reality of my disappointment. The author had not yet mastered the art of milking the scene. Specifically, she hadn't taken me *inside* the character's visceral experience of the action—the tension, the fear, the near-defeat, the barely achieved triumph—how all of that *felt*. Meanwhile, the anticlimactic climax dulled my enthusiasm for this author's work in general.

A writer's first imperative is to keep pages turning, to pull the reader into the story with such irresistible force he can't tear himself away. The second imperative is to provide this same riveted reader with a viscerally satisfying reading experience. Having pulled the reader into the scene, the author must then allow the reader to experience the events and emotions of that scene to the max. The author must milk the scene.

I've experienced few fictional narratives, in any medium, where this technique is more effectively practiced than in the tornado scene of the film *Places In the Heart*, written and directed by Robert Benton. This scene occurs just past the story's midpoint. The several major characters, and their deeply conflicted interactions, are already well established. The protagonist, Edna Spalding, flawlessly played by Sally Field, has reached a personal turning point. She's spanked her son for the first time and vows it will be the last, a decision that marks a deep change in her as a person and as a character.

Edna has further challenged prevailing wisdom in previous scenes. She's told that, given her husband's untimely death, she should accept a diminished future for herself and her two children. She can sell the family farm and live with relatives, or she can split up the family. Either way, she'll be dependent on others, a role that was considered appropriate for a woman in her position during the Great Depression era. Edna rejects this passive role. She is determined to save her farm.

Meanwhile, the vow never to spank her son again represents an even more profound break with tradition and her own history. She is rejecting her beloved late husband's way of doing things in favor of what seems right to her. Then, suddenly, as if nature herself is rising in protest against Edna's breach of gender and class expectations, the storm signs begin.

A stiffening wind whips the curtains inward from the windows of the beauty parlor run by Edna's sister, Margaret. Her patrons react with some surprise. This surprise is, as Jessica Lange instructed, their first and simplest genuine emotion in response to the approaching storm. Other emotions build naturally from there, as does the power of the wind, its sound and fury, through a montage of scenes switching among venues, each involving a central figure in the story.

Edna and her hired hand, Moze, struggle to move a frightened mule to the barn in the rising wind. Viola, the schoolteacher who's having an affair with Margaret's husband, herds children to what she hopes will be a safe section of the school building. Edna's blind boarder, Mr. Will, hears her young daughter, Possum, crying and gropes to find where she's hidden herself inside the Spalding farmhouse. On the road from town, Possum's slightly older brother, Frank, refuses a ride to a kindly neighbor's place. "I have to get home," he hollers into the mounting force of the wind.

These scenes shift back and forth, tension escalating with each shift: Human beings versus nature at her most fierce and arbitrary. Details of landscape disappear in a flurry of flying debris. The hasp strains on the door to the storm cellar where Edna, her children, Mr. Will and Moze have taken refuge. The schoolhouse collapses. There's little dialogue, only the deafening roar of the storm. I've heard a tornado described as sounding like a freight train. Robert Benton directs this scene to bear that out.

Benton also has written the scene to reveal character. Mr. Will reveals the kindliness beneath his curmudgeon exterior. Moze reveals that the shuffling, head-bowed deference demanded of his race masks a natural affinity for command. Edna reveals just how much she will risk, including her life, to save her family. We've seen evidence of these qualities in these characters before this scene. The storm simply casts them in stark, dramatic relief. If we, as viewers, had time or inclination for thought amidst our total, breathless immersion in this scene, we'd know that, when this storm is over, each of these characters and their circumstances will be changed.

Benton has taken us into the storm and made us not only witness that storm, but live it along with his characters. The entire scene is permeated with rising tension and heightened urgency, but nothing happens too abruptly. Events unfold at a steady, relentless pace. We long to know what will happen, but our progress toward that knowledge is delayed. We're jolted from one venue to another and another, until the pitch of our need to know the outcome is tuned as taut as the pitch of the tornado itself. At the same time, the story's characters are being tested by the intensity of what is happening to them, and their true underlying natures are indelibly revealed.

In your novel, the storm may be less literal, as in stormy external situations or turbulent internal ones. The need to wring every ounce of drama and tension from each scene still prevails. Temper that dramatization with Lange's admonition to begin with the simplest true and authentic emotion and build naturally from there, and you will avoid the danger of lapsing into melodrama. Melodrama does not build on genuine emotions that evolve from the true struggles of the human heart, but builds on overblown and contrived emotionalism calculated to manipulate the responses of the reader.

Simply show us what happens in the scene, blow by blow, both emotionally and physically. In real life, most intense moments happen very fast. In fiction, you must stretch that moment out, taking longer to tell it than the events would take in real life. This is called a time paradox, and must be accomplished while giving us the sense of things moving swiftly and under pressure. Robert Benton does that by cutting back and forth among highly charged scenes, which heightens our sense of time racing.

You, as author, can similarly quicken the pace at which the reader reads. Write in short, clipped sentences and short paragraphs that dash along the page. Or, present an especially tense passage as one long, breathless sentence. Be careful not to overuse these techniques. They are devices and, as such, are artificial. A device repeated too often becomes obvious to the reader, waking that reader from the dream of the story by making him aware of how the story is being told. The reader should only be aware of *what* is being told. And don't forget to take us inside the feelings of the characters. That emotional landscape is the true center of the story. Keep your focus there while you are milking the scene.

Crossroads

AN AUTHOR SELF-INTERROGATION

Ask yourself the following questions in reference both to the specific scene you are writing and to your novel as a whole. Your writerly instincts—again, trust me, you do have them—will tell you what choices you must make to strengthen your scene and your story. Check back through this passage for guidance. But, first of all, listen to those instincts of yours. Once you come to recognize your instinct's cadence and pay attention to its message, it will almost never steer you wrong.

1. What does your main character want in this scene?
2. What is this character willing to do to get what she wants? (In answering both of these questions, keep in mind what mystery author Elmore Leonard says: Everybody wants the same thing—to be happy, and to get what will make him happy. In other words, we all want to be satisfied. This is true of all characters, including the bad guys.)
3. Answer these first two questions for each pivotal character in the scene.
4. What stands in the way of your main character's goal in this scene and creates conflict as the character resists this opposition?
5. Do we know for certain which character's consciousness we are in here? Do we remain in this single consciousness throughout the scene, or at least throughout a significant segment of the scene? (Keep in mind that this is the most effective and stylistically sophisticated way of handling point of view in fiction.)
6. Do we see action and reaction between characters? Is each naturally and genuinely surprised by what the other says or does? Or do they seem to have anticipated what comes next, as if they'd read the script?
7. In dialogue, is there ever a question about which character is speaking? (If so, you risk confusing the reader and, thus, waking her from the dream of the story.)

8. Is what is being said in this dialogue interesting, compelling, riveting, maybe even startling? Or is it off-hand or insignificant?

9. What is the action of the scene? What is actually happening, as opposed to what is being said or thought? Is there enough action to keep the scene from dragging into stasis?

10. Does something unexpected happen in this scene? (Perhaps new information is added to the mix, or seeds of further conflict are planted between characters, or more questions are created in the reader's mind.)

11. Is there subtext beneath what is being said and done on the surface of the scene? (For example: Do the characters say one thing but think another? Do they show subtext by body language or tone of voice? Do they do something that could be interpreted more than one way?)

12. Does each character's situation change from the beginning to the end of the scene? What are the specifics of that change? Do the relationships between the characters also change? What are the specifics of these changes?

13. What is the outcome of this scene? Has the main character succeeded in achieving what she wanted? How has this character changed position in relationship to her ultimate goal in the story? (Keep in mind that if these changes—and the ones in the four previous questions—haven't happened in this scene, the work of the scene has not been done.)

14. Have you overwritten this scene? For example: Have you used unnecessary intensifiers, such as melodramatic verbs, too many adjectives, overwrought punctuation, or overdone dialogue? Have you portrayed overblown emotions with the main purpose of jerking an emotional response from the reader, rather than revealing the character's emotional truth?

Are You There Yet?

A HANDS-ON EXERCISE

Choose a highly dramatic, emotionally charged scene—preferably one you've not yet written—from the story you are developing. Craft (think about this for a while) a gem of an opening line for this scene—one that is compelling, concise, maybe even startling. Now write the scene at white-hot pace all the way through. This pace will not only keep you riveted to the writing of the scene, it will keep your eventual audience riveted to the reading of it, as well. Don't concern yourself consciously with the rules and principles implied by the questions in the previous segment of this passage. Trust your subconscious to have absorbed these principles on some level, and trust your writer's instinct to put them into practice now.

After you've completed this first draft of the scene, set it aside for at least a day. When that cooling-off period has lapsed, test this draft against the questions in the cossroads segment of this passage. Answer each question at length in your writer's journal. Let your impressions and responses flow freely. Further test your scene against the other principles of scene writing explored in this passage. How, specifically, does your scene measure up? How does it not?

Don't castigate yourself for those instances in which your scene falls short of what you'd like it to be. This is the revision phase, where the purpose is to discover such shortfalls and bring them up to speed. Do not become discouraged. Writing is a process, as is the progress of a writing career. If you apply yourself with genuine diligence to your work, and if you are serious about growing as a writer, you will do just that, with each scene and each story. I guarantee it.

Passage 7

THE MIDDLE OF THINGS—
DRAMA OR DOLDRUMS?

The structure of a novel in a nutshell sounds pretty simple. You start with a time, a place, and a story situation. The three basic elements of that situation are: a protagonist with reader appeal, a dilemma for that protagonist that erupts at the outset of the story and provides a goal plus motivation to act, and a character or circumstance that conflicts strongly with your protagonist's goal and intensifies the drama of your story. That's the opening.

The middle sounds even simpler. Obstacles arise to your protagonist's goal and must be overcome. Then comes the end where, in commercial fiction at least, the protagonist's conflicts are resolved. For a satisfying popular fiction ending, those conflicts will most often resolve in favor of the protagonist. In other words, as I've heard this structure even more pithily defined: you put your heroine up a tree; you throw rocks at her; you get her out of the tree. So, what's the big deal?

I've been asked a variation on that question about romantic fiction. Girl meets boy. Girl loses boy. Girl gets boy back again. What's the big deal? I always answer: Okay, you've recited the formula—now come up with three or four hundred pages of fascinating story to go with it. The same applies to the structuring of any novel, whatever the genre or category. All of it is a big deal, from captivating beginning to satisfying end. The biggest deal, when it comes to a storytelling challenge, is the middle.

Secret #31: Keep a Tight Grip on Your Story Line

You concoct a boffo opening for your story and your main character, as detailed in a previous passage. Meanwhile, as you begin to write this story, it is also desirable for you to know how it will end. This ending may change and evolve as you write, but the general direction should be clear to you from the outset. Otherwise, you can waste a lot of time in digressions that distract from and compete with your story line. These digressions, along with most other story line problems, occur in your middle chapters.

You've snagged the reader with the hook at the beginning of the story. You've jumped straight into the action at a point where the excitement and conflict have already commenced or are about to. You've startled the reader with a surprising situation. You've given just enough background information to let us know where we are, what's going on and, briefly, who the characters are. Now what?

I don't mean to belittle the process of coming up with a riveting opening. In order to explode into a story, you must have firepower. Coming up with that power is no small task. Still, I believe the true storytelling challenge is what comes next: keeping the narrative hook firmly planted in the reader and in the story taut, from the end of that boffo beginning to the beginning of the equally boffo end. The following are instructional examples of two authors mired in the middle.

Protagonist Crystal's story is a mystery novel. The author remains appropriately aware of this through the opening scenes. A body is discovered. Possible murder suspects are introduced. Crystal reveals herself as the amateur sleuth character. All of that is accomplished in fairly tight order. The reader, most often a fan of the genre, expects the story to continue along this vein with an investigation into the murder. Unfortunately, as the middle section of the story arrives, the author appears to forget what sort of book she is writing. Specifically, the amateur detective does almost no detecting. Instead, she jaunts off on one tangent, then another, some of them interesting, but none of them advancing the story. More suspects, leads, and clues are required, but they fail to emerge. The reader is left to detect where the mystery plot has gone.

In this manuscript, not only the thread of the mystery story is dropped. The development of Crystal's personal story falls by the wayside, as well. The opening scenes establish forward momentum along both of these story strands. Discoveries are revealed that complicate the mystery and add layers to the character. Suddenly, by the third chapter, we're off on one entirely different track after another. I suspect the author is attempting to create a montage effect of short, divergent scenes. This might work at a point of intense action in a much faster-paced story, like the film *Places In the Heart*, detailed in the previous passage. But even then, the technique demands extremely tight writing, the object being to create a progression of story punches that all but knock the reader out with their impact.

None of this happens in Crystal's story. The writing is loose. The punches fall short of or glance off their intended targets. The style of this story is more a cozy whodunit puzzle than the kind of hard-hitting thriller where action montages can be most effective. The author may mean to pull the story taut through the middle chapters, but instead the story meanders and slackens while the narrative hook lets go of the reader and is frittered away.

Here's an example of this author's mid-book misjudgments:

Crystal takes a trip that has only a tangential connection to the mystery plot. The character moves geographically from one place to another, but the story stands still. Plus, the author sacrifices the continuity of place that could help hold her story together. The scene is far too long, despite a few informational details, to justify its inclusion. If an event during the trip intensifies the mystery story, the scene could work. But this author needs to find a shorter, less convoluted means of revealing the information involved.

In the second problematic manuscript, the author of protagonist Mickey's story also loses his grip on the story line, albeit in a more intense passage than was the case with Crystal. Mickey's digression is intense because it is passionately written and, obviously, passionately felt by the author. His digression takes us to the Vietnam War, a subject with powerful emotional resonance for many readers. The author creates a scene that vibrates with this resonance. He has a tale he is compelled to tell, and he portrays that tale vividly.

But this novel has absolutely nothing to do with the Vietnam War. There is no logic to its inclusion here. Every story has its own world, and that world has rules. One of those rules is that every scene, every element, must fit logically into the overall world. Every scene must deepen our grounding in that world in some way. This author has left that ground and abandoned, however temporarily, the world of the book. He has let us off the hook of one story and snagged us with the hook of another, and now he expects us to be back on the original story again. The very intensity of this digressive scene defeats that expectation.

The author has jolted us out of the story established by his opening chapters. He does his best to pull us back into the story following the Vietnam detour, but he fails. He sacrifices the forward movement of the story by slipping into the memories of his two most significant characters. The author attempts a time layering effect here, which is another technique best suited to a different kind of book, perhaps a literary novel. In commercial fiction, which this story purports to be, a straightforward chronology is preferable. Maybe, if these memory elements were much shorter, they could be worked in throughout the story. As written, they turn the middle of this story into a muddle.

Both of these authors take the same wrong turn. Although they travel that detour at different speeds, they both let loose the tautness of their story lines. They build up momentum in tightly written opening scenes, then squander it in the middle of the story. They also squander our identification with the characters. We lose patience with Crystal because she doesn't follow through on her initial motivation to seek the murderer relentlessly. Mickey, on the other hand, bewilders us. We expect a journey through one story world, but we are lurched into another. Either way, we, as readers, have been cast adrift without a story line to grab hold of. Sooner or later, we float off, vowing never to revisit the work of these authors again.

Secret #32: What a Drag! Is Anything Happening Here?

Mid-book problems are often a matter of pacing. The examples in the previous secret have to do with the inclusion of too many digressions, details, and time shifts. The pace is slowed by scenes that are overstuffed rather than sleek and streamlined. Equally often, mid-book pacing problems have to do with the inclusion of too little— too little plot, too little event. There simply isn't enough going on to keep us eagerly turning pages. We no longer care what happens next, because nothing is happening now.

For example, a story involving protagonist Stack is supposed to be about a hardboiled character whose primary instinct should be to gravitate toward action. Instead, halfway through the very detailed synopsis, there's been only one tense, dramatic scene. This scene involves Stack and another character who is causing him trouble and even attempts to do him physical harm. Otherwise, the challenges to Stack are all verbal. He sits at a bar, trading sharp remarks with his sidekick. What could be more static than that? Some arguing happens. The author apparently thinks arguing is conflict. But the engagement between two arguing characters is never more than words. Anger may underlie the exchange, but I'm compelled to ask: "Will this anger lead to true conflict that will generate action and event in this story?" The answer is no. This forces me to ask an even more crucial question: "Does this author have a novel here?" Again, the answer is no.

Stack's story doesn't stack up. The author lets the drama fizzle out. The focus of that drama has to be a character in trouble. We never feel that Stack is in real trouble. His author shows us how tough and smart-mouthed Stack can be, but never reveals any of the humanity that might make him vulnerable to threat and, thus, more interesting to a reader. Stack is never in hot water, never really at risk. Consequently, his story loses steam.

What should this author have done? First and foremost, he should have been thinking cinematic. The story must have dramatic impact to hook the reader and the editor, and to keep them hooked. In commercial fiction in particular, the author's job is to come up with a strong story idea, then translate that idea into precise action that communicates the story to the reader with maximum clarity. Author and reader share the story. One way to do this is to define your story line and stick to it. Another way is to think of your story as a movie.

In popular cinema, as in popular fiction, the primary elements are talk and action. Watching popular films is a practical way to study the story structure that works for the mass marketplace. Look beyond the arresting opening, disregard the climactic close, and focus on what happens in between. Analyze the middle scenes. Study high-action classics like *Jaws* and *The French Connection*. Analyze more personal human stories, such as *The Verdict*, *Places In the Heart*, and other character-driven films. These movies were all blockbusters at the box office, and they all have a lot more than slam-bam action going for them.

What gives these stories wide-ranging appeal? For one thing, they are all David versus Goliath stories in which a lone character faces an overwhelming adversary. Each character is fighting for a righteous cause within the context of the individual story. Each has internal problems or limitations to overcome. If he doesn't overcome these, he will contribute to his own defeat, and very nearly does. These characters are alone because friends and allies have deserted them deliberately or due to an intervening circumstance, such as death. These characters are called upon to summon all their courage, both morally and physically, beyond any strength they dreamed they might possess. This courage makes them tenacious. Despite harrowing setbacks, they keep struggling to the triumphant end.

Many extremely successful screen scenarios incorporate these same elements. Call it a formula if you wish, but that would be simplistic and naïve. Coming up with specific details of character, situation, and motivation requires talent, imagination, and scads of adaptive creativity. What does persist—the relentless, unchanging absolute that could be thought of as a formula for story success—is conflict. Without conflict, there is no story interest, no story tension, no suspense regarding how the story will turn out. This conflict acts itself out through the middle chapters of the story, where it must occur in every scene and on every page. Scenes and pages without conflict are expendable.

Conflict is the key to creating, concocting, and imagining the kind of events and scenes that will avoid the bogged-down middle in any story, including Stack's. If his author had employed the mental energy required to evolve his scenes and events, there'd have been a compelling story to tell.

At the risk of condemnation for reducing storytelling to formula, I offer a list of a dozen suggestions for establishing and developing more than enough conflict and conflicted scenes to prop up any nothing-happening-here sag that may threaten the middle of your tale.

1. Think of the endless fundamental conflict between good and evil and how that universal conflict might manifest in your story.

2. Give each of your major characters a secret, a hidden goal, or guilt that creates internal conflict for the character.

3. Have these secrets and guilt feelings cause your characters to behave in mysterious and suspenseful ways that lead to external conflict in the story.

4. Employ the not-quite-enough-to-go-around principle. Each major character wants something that belongs to somebody else. Concentrate on providing excitement whenever you can, as long as it evolves naturally out of the characters and circumstances of the story.

5. Keep your characters talking. Make each verbal interchange an event by including real conflict in either the text or subtext of that conversation. Tighten the pace of these exchanges by avoiding interruptions to the flow of talk, such as internalizing thoughts or

over-describing characters' manners of saying what they say. Write your dialogue with so much conflict it speaks for itself.

6. Use the emotions of your characters, rather than their thoughts, to intensify situations and the conflicts in them. Facilitate this process by revisiting similar emotions in your own personal experience. Transport yourself back into an emotional place, noting the physical feelings, thoughts, behaviors, and changes. Conjure specific scene details and elements to illustrate these emotions in concrete terms.

7. Brainstorm additional dangers for your main characters from several directions. Make absolutely certain these dangers arise naturally and believably from the characters, their motivations, and the story's circumstances. Never impose these dangers artificially into the situation for the sole purpose of beefing up plot.

8. As you write the middle of your story, always keep the ending in mind. Think about mistakes your characters could make that would impede their progress, thus creating more conflict.

9. Remind yourself continually to avoid too much description. Instead, focus on creating exciting story scenes of purposeful talk and compelling action.

10. Further remind yourself to avoid giving information unless it is needed to understand the immediate story. Otherwise, you slow the action.

11. Remain intent upon making your characters' dilemmas worse to keep the pace of your scenes from dragging.

12. Never forget that you are depicting a protagonist with courage and inner strength. Know how she got that way. Confront this character with one jam after another, in which she will fight (not run away), confront (not surrender), stand up for what she believes, and do what must be done.

Secret #33: Factor in the Suspense Factor

An editor of popular fiction is looking for stories with the narrative power to keep readers turning pages. Much of that page-turner quality comes from suspense, which must exist in every novel, whatever the genre. Suspense evokes the question: "What's going to happen next?" In literary fiction, that question can be a matter of quiet curiosity underlying the reader's primary concern with the characters and who they are. In popular or commercial fiction, that question must be a compulsion.

The reader absolutely has to find out what is going to happen in this story. The worm of dissatisfaction will gnaw at him till he does. If he lost the book, he'd run out and buy another copy just to find out how the story ends. Would a reader feel that strongly compelled if he lost your book? Maybe, if he'd just finished reading your gripping opener or the equally involving couple of chapters following that opener, your story hook would be planted firmly enough to send him scurrying for a replacement copy.

But, what if this reader had read past that point to the middle of your book? Would your story still have its hooks so deep in him he'd be haunted by the need to know what happens next? Or, would he shrug his shoulders and not really care? The answer to these questions has everything to do with how well you, as author, have understood and employed the storytelling techniques of heightening narrative suspense in the middle chapters of that narrative. We've already discussed putting your characters in dire circumstances, embedding secrets and lies in your plot, and placing your characters in conflicted romantic relationships. Here are a few more of these techniques to heighten suspense:

Race Against Time: Increase the tension of your story situation by creating a time-defined demand on the characters, especially your protagonist. The most crucial goal of the story must be accomplished, in a specific and severely limited period of time. If it is not, terrible consequences will result, the more terrible the better. As the end of the designated time period draws near, story tension mounts. Obstacles to the goal, each one squandering valuable time, are written into the story. If the protagonist is to triumph, as should be the case in most popular fiction scenarios, that triumph will happen in the very last seconds of the allotted time.

On-Stage Drama: All intense scenes take place on the page, rather than off. Never avoid acting out important occurrences, especially the most uncomfortable ones. Keep the pace strong and relentless in your middle chapters by incorporating these kinds of intense, even disturbing events with vivid dialogue and action. Never tell the reader about something exciting or startling that has happened in your story. Show it to us as it is happening.

Narrow Escapes: Many of these devices—dire circumstances, secrets and lies, a race against time, scenes of intense drama—create opportunities for narrow escapes, which also are staples of the fast-paced story. Your protagonist, and once in a while your antagonist, is placed in jeopardy of losing everything, perhaps even life itself. The tension of this looming fate is drawn out to the point of near explosion. Then, by some clever and surprising means, the character escapes disaster at the absolute last minute and by the narrowest of margins. You can only get away with doing this once in the middle chapters of your story. Don't strain reader credulity by using any one of these plot-thickening techniques more often than is feasible for your story situation.

Cliffhangers: Practice ending chapters and scenes at moments of unanswered questions or unresolved suspense. Your protagonist is approaching or suddenly confronted with a threat of some kind. This danger, whatever it may be, is not yet completely realized. The chapter or scene ends before that realization occurs. The danger may fully materialize in the next scene, or be forestalled by the intervention of a scene, or scenes, involving a separate though relevant situation at a different time and place. In either case, the reader is cast into a state of anticipation, needing to know what happens next. As with all of these techniques, the cliffhanger must evolve naturally from the story situation. Never create an artificial cliffhanger situation for the mere purpose of inventing an atmosphere of panic and tension. Such contrivances are always storytelling blunders.

These are all legitimate strategies for intensifying your story's suspense factor by maintaining strong pacing at its middle stages. Employ them all, as they apply, for the enrichment of your story. However, I caution you against another, not at all legitimate plot device. This device, too often found in eminently rejectable manuscripts, is the misunderstanding between characters that doesn't stand up to tests of logic and good story sense. If this misunderstanding could be resolved by a simple conversation between these characters, it will not survive such scrutiny. If this misunderstanding takes the form of a misjudgment of one character by another, make certain the erroneous opinion is strongly motivated and believable. Otherwise, the portrayal of the misjudging character could be compromised. Misunderstandings only work when they grow, as I've said so many times before, naturally and believably from story situation and character. Only then can they add to the suspense of your story.

Secret #34: Heat the Pot for the Reader

The secret of the page-turner novel is emotional impact on the reader. At the beginning of the story, this impact is created by the initial appeal of a compelling combination of character and situation. At the end of the story, a strong climax must be at least equally powerful. In between, the challenge is to sustain that emotional impact. This requires intensity in all aspects of the writing. I've mentioned intensity before, but it takes on added importance in the middle of the story.

Intensity of Characterization:

1. Begin with the protagonist because this person is someone we respond to positively—someone we like and admire and want to see win. This character is a heroic figure, and we naturally, intensely support heroism.

2. Next, as foil to this hero, you need a worthy heroine. This opposite-gender role can be filled by a romantic partner, non-romantic partner, or sidekick. This first among secondary characters has her own kind of appeal to the reader. For example, the heroine in a romantic relationship with the hero protagonist is the kind of woman a reader will fall in love with. In a non-romantic relationship, she is the kind of character we like or are amused by. Whatever your choice, there must be obstacles and conflicts in this relationship to give it impact.

3. Finally, the antagonist must be someone we dislike as much as we like the protagonist. Therefore, the reader has a personal, emotional, intense stake in the antagonist's defeat.

Intensity of Plot: There is a great deal at stake in this story. Terrible consequences will occur if your protagonist fails. Lots of conflict ensues, trouble intensifies, never flags, in the middle chapters. That conflict grows worse and worse, all the way to the climactic scene, and pulls the reader along with its intensity.

Intensity of Presentation: The story is written in strong scenes, like a movie, with brief transitions between these scenes. The effect is like the jump cuts in a film, with the pacing pulled along relentlessly from scene to scene, each containing conflict, each exciting in its own right. Before writing a scene, ask yourself, How can I make this situation more exciting? After writing the scene, ask yourself the same question once again. A dull scene that doesn't move either reader or plot doesn't belong in your story, especially in the middle of that story where maintaining strong pacing is crucial.

To find the intensity in your story, you must first seek the emotional truth of that story. The writer must wear his heart on his sleeve or, more accurately, wear his heart on the page. Getting to the emotional truth of a story has everything to do with a valorous pursuit, a willingness to be vulnerable in what you write. It takes courage to reach down inside yourself, find your heart as the conduit to the heart of your characters, and tell it like it is—like it is for you.

Your own humanity is your avenue, your vehicle, for reaching and writing stories that readers and editors will care about all the way through. The object of such writing is to stay with the feelings of the character. This emotional priority affects the storytelling choices you make—the kind of character you write, what that character's actions and reactions will be, and the specific events or scenes you select to portray that character. Base these choices on this question: What will dramatize the emotional truth of this story most effectively or, in other words, with greatest impact?

Impact comes from engaging emotions, both the reader's and your own. An emotionally charged story, when paired with intense portrayal of the feelings involved, is the key to hooking the reader. But first you must hook yourself. If the story isn't beating in your heart, it can't come truly alive in your head or on paper. Start at your gut, and at the gut of your characters. Dig for the raw feelings. Unearth, explore, reveal, and rejoice in them. They are storytelling pay dirt.

One path to those feelings is paved by sense memory, your own specific experiences with these emotions in your own life. Ask yourself, What experience in my life has called up the most intense instance of this emotion? Climb inside that memory with all your senses primed. Think, breathe, and feel yourself back into that moment. Write what you find there. If there is pain involved, don't push it away. Write the pain out onto the page. Pain is intensity, that storytelling pay dirt I've been talking about.

Writing fiction is a dangerous activity. When you tell the truth, you take risks. When you tell emotional truth, the most threatening truth of all, you take great risks. You threaten others with exposure to the intensity of life. You threaten yourself with exposure of the self beneath your persona. Emotionally truthful writing at its most powerful is often uncomfortable to write. It requires the audacity to create the world of your book in terms that ring emotionally true and strike emotionally deep. All of these emotions begin inside you and end up on the page, in your characters. Here's how to make that happen in your story:

1. Place your protagonist under stress to bring out the true nature of her character, her emotional truth.
2. Make sure this results in a highly dramatic story situation with physical or emotional danger to your protagonist. Intensify that

danger through the middle of the story, heightening the emotional stakes for your protagonist.

3. Give your protagonist an overwhelming motivation to stay—her need, plus intense emotional undertones—stronger than any peril that may cause her to want to flee. This motivation gives your story its driving narrative force into and through its middle chapters.

4. Make your protagonist's motivation reflect and reveal her emotional priorities—what she most intensely wants and needs—at the core of her personal emotional truth.

5. Make obstacles arise at just about every turn so that your protagonist must keep struggling to achieve her goal.

6. Make sure your protagonist has human flaws that are as much a part of her emotional truth as her strength. The intensity of the story situation must exacerbate these flaws, her fears in particular. How your protagonist handles these fears throughout the middle of the story reveals her character at its deepest, truest level.

7. Create a primary relationship in your story that is also an emotional quagmire. The issues between your protagonist and this other character should create additional conflict and intensify the emotional stakes of the story, revealing her true emotional character.

All of the above is about getting to the underneath of your character, and through her, to the underneath of your story—the emotional truth that lies beneath the surface and affects everything that happens there. Experiment with these tips by writing a scene that belongs in the middle of your book. Put your protagonist in action by employing each of the seven elements above. Remind yourself that your overriding purpose is to unearth and reveal the emotional truth. Then, put that thought out of your head and just write.

Secret #35: Writing Love Scenes and Loving It

Take two people strongly attracted to one another, add internal and
external obstacles to their getting together, and you have a formula
for conflict and emotional intensity. If these two characters are
adults in fiction, sex is bound to be involved. In some stories, there
may be only sexual tension that is never acted upon. In a contemporary story, however, you need to be cautious about this scenario.
The priority is to tell the truth, the whole truth, and nothing but
the truth. The whole truth of most contemporary adult lives is that,
when sexual attraction arises between two of those contemporary
adults, consummation occurs.

This brings us to writing what too many people call the sex
scene. I prefer the term love scene. Sex with, rather than without,
love appeals most widely to female readers, the audience segment
that buys the most popular fiction. In my experience, manuscripts
with well-written love scenes are rare. Most are badly written, and
most of those are overwritten. My personal least favorite example
of love scene overwriting: "He sipped at her lips." Try visualizing
that. Such writing invites ridicule. The author has mistaken melodrama for passion.

The opposite sin is a form of underwriting that denies, even
insults the humanity of the lovers. My least favorite example here
refers to the most intimate moment of a love scene as one lover
having "entered" the other, as if she were a door or a contractual
agreement. Unless you're writing a police report or a trial testimony
transcript, this form of expression is way too detached and loveless
for most readers.

The overly detailed but perfunctory love scene is both too much
and too little. Too many physical moves are described—whose hands

are where doing what, what is being mouthed by whom. The effect is clinical at best, crude at worst. At the same time, too little consideration is given to the humanity of the lovers, this time in favor of an attempt to titillate the reader. I'm reminded of the contrast between a porno film and the scene between Deborah Kerr and Burt Lancaster on the beach in *From Here to Eternity*.

All of the above love scene mishaps reflect the author's discomfort with human sexuality. He has distanced himself from the lovemaking of his characters. Instead of portraying that potentially powerful event from the inside, the author removes himself to a safe, less embarrassing, less personally revealing distance, and observes. Whether that observation is too overheated or too dispassionate, the essence of the error is the same. The author has failed to portray the genuine emotional experience of the characters.

Once you've decided to include adult sexuality in your story, consider your attitude toward that sexuality. That attitude, and the fine-tuning of it, will determine whether or not your love scene succeeds. That is, whether or not it appeals to the majority of readers in the audience you need to reach. A love scene that succeeds is one you're proud of once you have written it.

Love scenes can be wonderfully erotic, enriching to the story, and intense. Or, they can jar the reader by coming across as inserted to satisfy an assumed formula. Too many writers reach a point in their story where they intend a love scene to occur and then put off writing that scene. Later on, sometimes after the book is finished, they return to that section and write a love scene to be inserted there. These scenes often fail to integrate as well as they should into the surrounding action, the character development, or the tone and feel of what is going on right then in the story.

Love scenes can be sensually written, exciting all of the senses by making the reader feel what the characters are feeling. Or, they can be rife with melodramatic or overly harsh clichés that distract from the storytelling. Love scenes can be the stuff of romantic fantasy and, at the same time, the stuff of reality. Or, they can be schmaltzy, embarrassing, and, worst of all, devoid of love.

Love scenes devoid of love are about taking instead of giving, self-gratification instead of sharing, lust instead of passion. They are rapacious rather than loving. They are about power rather than empowerment. The majority of love scenes are written for a female readership. That readership responds most positively to sexual love that is giving, sharing, passionate, loving, and empowering—in real life and books alike.

When I lecture on this subject, at just about this moment in my presentation somebody asks, "Do I *have* to include sex in my novel?" I respond, "Nobody *has* to do anything. But if you intend to write authentically about adult life, it will be difficult to do so without portraying the sexuality of your characters." You sacrifice audience appeal when you choose to circumvent the narrative tension of sexual attraction and the conflict-rich relationship possibilities that go with it.

It is equally unwise to include a love scene without first asking yourself, "How essential is a physical relationship to the story I'm telling?" If you are writing women's popular fiction, the answer will almost always be, "*Very* essential." Ask yourself, "How explicit must this scene be?" In popular fiction, that answer will almost always be, "As explicit as is necessary to make the scene intense."

You may also need to ask yourself, "How unconventional does the sex in my story have to be?" If you're writing commercial fiction meant to attract a wide female audience, that answer should almost always be, "Not particularly." Hot sex need not be degrading or exploitative. Hot sex can simply be hot. These two characters really want each other, right here, right now. A love scene is justified, in storytelling terms, when the reader shares in the intense emotional experience of the characters and learns something important from the scene. Here are some examples of what the reader might learn:

- That these two people absolutely belong together.
- That these two people belong together, but they have real problems.
- That these two people belong together, but they may not end up together.
- That these two people do not belong together. (If they are hero and heroine in most women's fiction, we will eventually see them as belonging together.)
- That these two people have certain characteristics that will be crucial to the development and resolution of the story.

Be careful not to overload the scene with too many of these elements. You are writing a love scene, after all. Your priority is to portray, sensually and authentically, the emotional and physical experience of your characters with a vividness that communicates this experience to the reader in the most powerful manner possible. With that in mind, let me very frankly say that there's nothing wrong with turning your reader on to the sexual feelings you depict. Nor, is there anything wrong with arousing yourself by the writing. These are the natural effects of writing sensual truth.

To be good storytelling, the scene must create story tension as well as sexual tension. The action in a love scene is very touchy, very personal. Even where there is love, maybe especially where there is love, there also must be conflict. No matter how attracted your two characters are to each other, something else crucial is at stake here for each of them. Their lives will be altered irrevocably by this encounter. The love scene enriches your story by complicating it even further than was previously the case.

Here are some precautions to keep in mind when planning and writing a love scene:

- Avoid false casualness, such as too much over-clever banter. The intense emotions of your characters should override this dialogue.
- Avoid too much physical description. The feelings are much sexier than the blow-by-blow action.
- Avoid coming across as uncomfortable. Sex is natural, healthy, and meant to be enjoyed. Check your neurotic inhibitions at your door.
- Avoid aimlessness. Know what is supposed to happen in this scene and why. Advance planning of the scene is essential.
- Avoid dragging along. Even the most sensual love scene grows tedious when it goes on too long or moves too slowly.
- Avoid making sex a power game where the woman is forced or defeated by the man. Such scenes exhibit an outdated attitude toward both sex and women.
- Avoid portraying male sexuality as force. A man who is lively and interesting with his clothes on shouldn't suddenly become cruel and brutal in bed—unless, perhaps, you are depicting a psychopath.
- Avoid consequences that portray sex as punishable. Don't have your contemporary novel characters suffer terrible fates for having relished sex.
- Avoid discussions of sexual diseases, condom use, and related subjects. Such references jolt the reader too starkly awake from the romantic reverie you are attempting to create, at least in most women's fiction.

- Avoid lovemaking that is inept and fumbling. No unsavory elements, such as body odors, should appear. The fantasy element so many readers crave is jeopardized by this degree of realism.
- Avoid character behaviors in this scene that are not consistent with the way these characters behave in the rest of the story.
- Avoid a purely lustful scene. Have your characters express physical affection and tenderness toward one another, as well.
- Avoid the feeling that we've heard this before. Take care not to let the language become pretentious or hackneyed or silly. Opt instead for strong, precise, vivid phrases. One false word, and the mood you are attempting to create can be destroyed.
- Avoid a "cut to the trees." Two characters share a passionate kiss. You "cut to the trees" in the form of a paragraph break and line space. The next paragraph begins after the encounter. You've taken the easy way out of a challenging writing situation. You've lost the opportunity to show us significant things about how your characters behave under intense emotional circumstances. You've omitted a scene that could be pivotal to your story's outcome. You may have been discreet, but you haven't told the strongest story possible.

Crossroads

AN AUTHOR SELF-INTERROGATION

When you feel your story losing its momentum in the middle chapters, ask yourself these questions to help build rising action.

1. Do I know everything I need to know about my characters?
   a. What hidden relationships could there be between them?
   b. What further conflict lies beneath the surface of my characters' relationships?
   c. What past secrets, previously unrevealed, do my characters have, and why?
   d. What secret purposes, previously unrevealed, do they have, and why?
2. How can I make my protagonist's situation more difficult, even intolerable?
   a. What additional misfortunes can befall this character?
   b. What can happen that would jolt this character?
   c. What can happen that would frighten this character?
   d. What potent and dangerous secrets surround this unwitting character?
3. What has happened in the past that could affect my present story?
   a. What actual historic events might I tie in to the story?
   b. What about the ancestry of my characters might I tie in?
   c. How are deceased characters affecting living ones?
   d. What powerful events in the past set present story events in motion?
4. How can I force my characters to make decisions that demand action?
   a. What situations already exist in my story that could demand such decisions?
   b. What further situations could I create that would demand such decisions?
   c. What drives do my characters have that they could further act upon?
   d. What action might one character take against another?

5. What further research might I do to generate more story material?
    a. What research might I do into the setting (time and place) of the story?
    b. What research might I do into the occupations of my characters?
    c. What plot possibilities does this further research open up?
    d. What could be mysterious, nefarious, or eerie here?
6. How might I use my life (and the lives of my friends) as story material?
    a. What have I felt deeply (angered, ecstatic, humiliated, terrified, guilty, anxious) about lately?
    b. How can I make my characters experience these same feelings?
    c. What events currently are happening to me that might fit into my story?
    d. What has happened to me in the past that might fit into my story?

Are You There Yet?

A HANDS-ON EXERCISE

I've adapted a version of my "Writing Characters From the Inside Out" exercise to writing love scenes. For this exercise, you will, of course, need two lovers. It would be preferable to use the hero and heroine of your present novel the first time you perform this exercise. If you don't have two such characters available in your present work, choose a pair from literature or film to experiment with. Be sure to select characters with sufficient story energy to come to life on the page. This exercise provides a means for you to become these characters and breathe that energy and life into them from the inside out. I repeat the instructions here for your information. A warning: The exercise items and the responses they elicit are of a sexually intimate and explicit nature. Proceed with that in mind.

WRITING LOVE SCENES FROM THE INSIDE OUT

1. Write in your writer's journal, responding to each item below.
2. Write in the first person, using "I."
3. Write *as* your character, not talking *about* her, but *being* her and speaking as her.
4. Concentrate on how you, as this character, are *feeling* about each item and how it relates to you. Answer from the *gut* of this character, not from the head. Minimize rumination, theorizing, and abstractions. Preferably, omit them altogether.

THE EXERCISE PREMISE

The imagination is sensual and powerful. Imagining is the first act of sexual foreplay, which begins and builds the arousal, and which may or may not be consummated soon (depending on the story). By employing the sexual imagination, you can hold off consummation and still write very erotic material.

THE EXERCISE—FIRST PHASE

Even before any lovemaking has happened between us, I have strong, physical feelings for this man.

Seeing him, fully clothed and at a bit of a distance. . . .

I find myself first attracted to his. . . .
I would most like to touch his. . . .
I can already imagine that he would feel like. . . .
I can already imagine that he would smell like. . . .

I can already imagine that he would taste like. . . .
When I imagine his arms around me, I feel. . . .
As I think about being close to him, being touched by him, I experience these sensations inside me. . . .
When I fantasize that he is naked with me, I see. . . .
When our naked bodies touch one another, they are. . . .
His hands on my body are. . . .
My hands on his body are. . . .
His mouth on my body is. . . .
My mouth on his body is. . . .
If I have thoughts in my mind at this moment, they are. . . .
As the moment nears when he will be inside me, I feel. . . .
When he is first inside me, all I want to do is. . . .
Making love, with him deep inside me, is. . . .
As we come to the release of climax together, I feel. . . .

THE EXERCISE—SECOND PHASE
As I think back over our lovemaking together, there are things I would have liked to say to him. I would like to say:

When he first puts his arms around me. . . .
After I first feel his lips on mine. . . .
When he first touches my body. . . .
When I first see him naked. . . .
When I first touch his body. . . .
When his lips first touch my body. . . .
After my lips first touch his body. . . .
As the moment nears when he will be inside me. . . .
As we move together in passionate frenzy. . . .

Now that our lovemaking is done (for the moment):

My body feels. . . .
My heart is. . . .
What I want to tell him is. . . .
What I want most is. . . .
What I will always remember is. . . .
[Add here anything further you, as the character, are feeling.]

THE EXERCISE—THE MALE PHASE

When "Writing Characters From the Inside Out" in the man's point of view, use the items listed in the technique described above. Respond to each item as this male character, substituting pronouns (she for he, etc.) where necessary.

If you are a woman writing as a man, remember that you are writing in a man's tone of voice, from a man's feelings and experience. If you are a man writing as a woman, remember that you are writing in a woman's tone of voice, from a woman's feelings and experience. Writing from the point of view of the opposite sex requires an imaginative leap. Remember that your first duty as a writer is to be true to this character, who and what he or she is and what lies in that character's heart, soul, and senses. You may want to enlist the counsel of a real-life person of the opposite sex . . . or you may not need to. As always, you must trust in your writer's imagination and the wonders it can and will perform.

Passage 8

STYLE IS NOT JUST FASHION

We've discussed the *why* of a novel—the idea. We've discussed the *who* of a novel—the characters. We've discussed the *what* of a novel—the plot. Now, we must discuss the *how* of a novel—the style. I deliberately insert this discussion here, before winding up our exploration of what/plot with a passage on writing endings and revising the whole, because I want to dissuade you from regarding style as an afterthought.

Writing style in a manuscript submission is, as the publishing business progresses, more and more a wheat-from-chaff element. An impressive number of authors continue to school themselves, formally and informally, in the techniques of idea development, characterization, and plotting. An increasing number of manuscripts reach the desks of editors and literary agents with those elements in a fairly sophisticated state. Meanwhile, the number of open slots on any given publisher's list continues to decrease.

In more generous times, a strongly characterized and plotted popular fiction story with a compelling central idea had a good chance of being published even if the writing style was less than polished. We've all read the results, stories frustrated us with their awkward writing but kept us turning pages anyway. We continue to find such stories on bookstore shelves, most often from authors who established a readership in that past, less persnickety era. In my opinion, many of those authors would not find a publisher today.

An editor deciding which titles to publish—or an agent deciding which authors to represent—is going to look beyond idea, character, and plot before declaring thumbs up or thumbs down. That editor or agent is going to look closely at writing style. Slipshod writing and slapdash style have little chance of making the cut in the current, more-competitive-than-ever publishing marketplace. As a reader, I'm pleased by this. As a writer, I'm struck numb with fear. You should be, as well.

The ante is up. You must write smoothly, with sophistication, in a compelling voice to be published now. That is true for the previously published novelist—unless that novelist has a large and loyal readership already committed to his work—as well as for the previously unpublished one. You must perform at your absolute best stylistically. And your best will have to be better than almost everybody else. Nothing less will do.

You must be extremely hard-nosed in determining whether your work is really that good or not. Check your ego at your office door. Let in only your most demanding editorial self. Listen to what she says. Her advice, as long as it is clear-eyed and true, could mean the difference between ending up on the wheat side of the divide and finding yourself on the refuse pile with the chaff.

Secret #36: Describe True to Life

It all comes down to selectivity. We begin with selectivity in description. Think in terms of your priorities—to be clear, concise, and clean in your writing. The author of Maxine's story was definitely not thinking in that vein. She apparently wanted to impress her readers with the beauty of her story setting. She goes on and on about that beauty, heaping up adjectives and adverbs along the way, so much that eventually I was ready to cry out, "Enough already. I get the picture. The place is beautiful. Please, get on with the story."

I told the author this, though in more diplomatic terms. She wailed that I was denigrating her best writing. She claimed I didn't appreciate her writing style, but this was not her best writing. It was her most self-indulgent writing. She'd fallen into the lyricism trap. Most of us, as novelists, spend some time there. What author has not written a passage and then preened, "This is so nice. This is so lovely." Writers of commercial fiction should beware of loveliness. It could be your stylistic downfall.

I'm not asking you to deny yourself the euphoria of writing these passages, however overblown or flowery they may be. Go ahead. Wallow in lyrical imagery, even sentimentality. But when you've gorged yourself and the page, go back and take it all out, every word. Remember you are trying for clear, concise, clean writing—the opposite of self-indulgent, overblown, and sentimental prose. The former is true to your scene. The latter is a distortion of that truth, which doesn't preclude description by any means. It does, however, prescribe that description must be selective. Think of yourself as a microscope, focusing closer and closer in on a scene or a character, putting yourself right into that scene or character. You are in search of a single, very specific detail. This is to be a concrete and realistic detail, one that the reader will react to emotionally and with recognition because it causes that reader to understand what is going on in the scene or with the character. The reader's mind is jogged by this detail, because it resonates with his own experience or one similar to it.

As readers, we learn most effectively and respond most readily to such emotion-laden images. As writers, our job is to stimulate these moments of recognition. Thus, we create an aura of realism around even the most fantastic story. Think of the writing of Stephen King. His use of brand-items and culturally common objects or experiences draws us into his stories and makes them real for us, however outlandish those tales may be. You can do the same with your writing by mastering use of closely observed details for each of your scenes and characters.

Choose these details with great care. The object is to capture the essence of the place or person or mood in a single detail. When you do so, you bring the reader close to the scene. You involve that reader in the scene. To do this, you must stop the forward movement of the writing for a moment. To get at this detail, you must travel to the depths of the scene or character. Remember the microscope. Stop and go down into the scene. Find the detail there, at the heart of the scene or character. Feel for that detail until it resonates for you as you intend it to resonate for the reader.

You only need one, or at most two, such details to bring a scene or character to life for the reader. Too many details obscure rather than clarify what you are describing. They cause the mind to glaze over. They are too much to take in. Think of the scene you are about to write. Visualize it. Search for the perfect details to re-create that vision for the reader, to make the scene come alive. Do the same with characters, making the essence of each one more concrete. Do this before writing, as well as during the writing process. Stay alert for the surprises that happen during this process and the resonant details that come to you as a result. Such details must be:

- Sensual, as in engaging the senses.
- Visual, so we actually see in our minds what is happening.

- Emotional, evoking a catch in the throat of the reader.
- Haunting, sticking in the reader's mind.
- Original, not giving us the sense of having heard this before.

Set aside a section in your writer's journal for recording these sensual, visual, emotional, haunting, original images as they occur to you. Also record these images when you come upon them in your reading, especially from the writings of great authors, who are, after all, our best teachers.

Secret #37: Keep Talking

As your reader reads, she's also listening. It is your job to make sure what she listens to is compelling. The worst of all writerly sins, in commercial fiction at least, is to bore your reader. For example, avoid droning on and on with interior monologue. You may find fascination in the uninterrupted narrative of your own thoughts, or those of your character, but others most likely will not. So, if your mandate is to give your reader a compelling reading/listening experience, what must you do? One choice is to write action, but too much of that without respite can become monotonous, as well. This is where dialogue comes in.

There is an art to writing good dialogue. You must master that art. Poorly written dialogue can be just as boring as long paragraphs of interior monologue. Exciting dialogue is spoken by smart characters saying important things. Beware of small talk, especially greetings, partings, and politesse. Avoid banter unless it has a clear and significant story purpose and suits the mood of what is happening between the speaking characters.

Remember the example of Maxine's story from earlier in this

passage? Maxine's author ignores these precautions, the one about significant dialogue content in particular. Her characters chat a lot, and they chat about subjects far afield from the story situation. When they begin to speak, the pace of the story slows to a crawl. This may be the kind of conversation we carry on in real life, but it has no place in fiction, where establishing and maintaining narrative tension are primary storytelling concerns. Each dialogue speech must have a purpose in the story—revealing character, moving action, providing needed information. The characters in Maxine's story too often simply babble on. Nothing is accomplished by their chatter, other than distancing the reader from the story.

These chattering characters also sound very much alike. There is little differentiation of one voice from another. Develop a knack for creating a distinct voice for each character by becoming a good listener. Adopt the habit of eavesdropping, as discussed in an earlier passage of this book. Listen for those qualities of individual speech that set it apart from the speech of other people—length of sentences, use of slang or colloquialism, choice of diction, tone, and attitude. This creates more fodder for your writer's journal. Take note of the things people say and how they say them. Make it a lifelong study, and never feel guilty about eavesdropping again.

Chat also has no subtext. Chat is only surface. Intriguing dialogue hides something beneath its surface from one or all parties involved in the conversation. The reader is privy to that hidden element—a secret, a lie, an occurrence, or even the presence of a clandestine listener. Much of the dialogue in Maxine's story has no subtext. No underlying contradictions or deeper implications create conflict and suspense. What you hear is what you get.

Maxine's author was also guilty of another dialogue writing mistake—too much rambling narrative. The character describes who she is by thinking about herself and narrating those thoughts on the page. She'd have been wiser to show us who she is via her dialogue, the things she says and how she says them. This is a much more effective and stylistically sophisticated way of revealing character than interior monologue could ever be. Write strong dialogue and trust it to carry this characterization burden.

Also, trust strong dialogue to require no description of itself. In Jed's story, the speaking characters testify, explain, exclaim, proclaim, jump in, propose, decipher, and remonstrate, plus a whole lot more. I ask this author, "What's wrong with good old he said, she said? Why not choose the words spoken with such care and specificity that the speech itself will make obvious the manner of speaking?" Description of dialogue disrupts the flow of conversation. Natural flow of conversation—things said in fiction as they could be said in real life—is the essence of well-written dialogue. Anything less is just blather, and badly blathered blather at that.

Dialogue also can be rendered ineffective by pretension. The characters in Carlotta's story talk like upper-class Brits, even though they don't have a drop of British blood among them. The sound of their speech is at best overly formal and at worst affected. One character says to another, "You're a caution." The response is, "Please, do go away, you vile monster." They use "one" to refer to self, as in, "One never knows." Which brings us to the worst thing about pretentious dialogue: It is irritating. The author may have been trying for eccentricity of conversational tone. Instead, her characters sound haughty. We're annoyed by them. And this bodes badly for the character identification storytellers must achieve.

This author then goes on to simulate African-American dialect. Surprisingly, considering the above examples from the same manuscript, this dialect sounds pretty authentic, but there is simply too much of it, so much that we're distracted from the story. We stop hearing *what* is being said because our heads are too full of the accent in which it is said. This illustrates that in dialogue you even can have too much of a good thing. Be sure to sound authentic, and then use only enough dialect to give the flavor of the characters' speech. This applies to foreign accents, actual foreign language phrases or any other departures from standard spoken American English.

Remember that what a character says and how he says it are crucial elements of his characterization. What he says reflects who he is, even when he's lying. Conversely, who this character is determines what he will say. Any out-of-character speech, like any out-of-character action, must be justified by a strong story purpose and some preparation, in the previous pages, for his deviation. Otherwise, your characters may be talking the talk, but they're not walking the walk.

Secret #38: Write Tight to Write Right

William Carlos Williams defined a well-written poem as one with no extra parts in it. A well-written novel is the same, nothing extraneous allowed. The writing is tight, contained, clear, and to the point. Such writing is at the heart, as well as in the surface style, of good contemporary storytelling. Archaic times may have permitted, even encouraged, ornate writing. Today's editors and literary agents are repulsed by it. When it comes to telling a modern story for a modern audience, cleanliness is next to godliness—as in, keep your writing squeaky clean.

Adopt a spare style. Avoid wordiness. Too many words erect a barrier between the reader and the emotional truth of the story. Too many words hold the reader back from the beating hearts of your characters. He must climb over those words to get to what truly matters, and that is too much to ask of him. Too many words are like too much description. They obscure the image you're trying to portray. The purpose of language is to transmit the story as directly as possible, from the consciousness of the writer to the consciousness of the reader. Employing language for any other purpose is a misuse of our most valuable storytelling tool. So, simplify, simplify, simplify.

I've talked about melodrama before. It's also an example of yet another form of reader abuse. Melodramatic writing messes with the reader's emotions, or tries to. The author of Megan's story means to engage the reader's sympathy by referring to a child as "a poor, forsaken creature" and to excite the reader's antipathy by referring to the villain as "a coldhearted beast." First, she tries to jerk our heartstrings. Next, she comes after our hatestrings. She doesn't trust her characters or their situation to capture our affections, or disaffections, on their own. She blows up the writing with the overheated air of overheated prose, and deflates our response in the process. This is the opposite of the less-is-more technique. We are turned off, rather than turned on, feeling as if the author meant to manipulate us.

Finally, the story must be as tightly composed as the prose in which it is written. John Roy makes a sudden decision to change the course of his murder investigation. That would be fine if he had a good reason for doing so. No such motivation is presented in his story as it was written and submitted to me. The story moves along a well-plotted path of cause and effect to this point. Suddenly, that plot cohesiveness is lost. The character takes off on a tangent, and we readers are loath to follow.

If we read John Roy's tale all the way to the end, which we now may not care to do, we can see the method in this authorial madness. The abrupt, unwarranted shift of story direction sets the author on course toward the ending he has calculated but not adequately plotted toward. Again, the reader is jerked toward accepting a less than logical conclusion to the story. The author has included an extraneous twist in the plot and loosened the tension of his story line by doing so. He should have stuck to his original storytelling guns as firmly as he expects his hardboiled private investigator to do.

Secret #39: Leave Your Smarty Pants in the Closet

Have you ever watched people trying too hard to make an impression? They strain to create the illusion of being something other than what they are. A talented actor, adept at his craft and savvy about his audience, creates this illusion convincingly. He resists the temptation to overact. A less talented actor does not. The talented actor's performance flows naturally into and through the character he portrays. We believe he is that character. We forget he's an actor playing a part. The less talented actor strains for an effect, and we see that straining. We're distracted from the character by the affectedness of the portrayal. The same is true in writing.

Remember Carlotta's story? The one with the pretentious dialogue? Unfortunately, the posturing doesn't stop, or start, there. This author begins each chapter with a long title, generally Victorian in tone. She follows that title with an even longer quotation from a literary work. Some of these quotations relate more directly to the ensuing chapter than others. All are a distraction from the story.

An eighteenth century author might begin her chapters with intrusive titles and quotations meant to foreshadow events to come. Her readers were accustomed to such interruptions to story flow. A contemporary reader is less patient, and justifiably so. The story's the thing, especially in popular fiction. Opening quotes halt the reader's progress through the story. She thinks about what the quote could mean in this context when she should be immersed in that context itself and thinking about nothing else.

Carlotta's author repeatedly wakes us, quite rudely, from the dream of her story. These rude awakenings occur whenever we are distracted from the story itself by our awareness of how the story is being told. The curtains have been pulled away from the theater arch. The ropes and battens and lighting fixtures are exposed. The dramatic illusion is compromised. This may be appropriate for an experimental play, or even experimental literature. Popular fiction is less tolerant of such interventions. Stick to the story without the distracting trimmings. Keep the reader immersed in the dream.

Carlotta's creator is not yet finished trying to impress us with her erudition. She peppers the text with obscure literary references. I can't cite the specific references without violating the anonymity of this author. If she explained these references, she might get away with them. But no explanations are offered, and they would most likely be more distracting digressions even if they were. This author's goal should have been to write a big-selling novel, not an idiosyncratic piece that would appeal only to a niche audience, leaving the majority of readers behind. Accessibility is key in popular fiction.

Ill-chosen literary devices can be even more distracting. The best way to tell most stories is straight up. An extraordinary manner of telling is problematic, unless the story cries out for it. We must be convinced, upon reading the story, that it absolutely could not be told as effectively any other way. The author of Peter's story chose to present his story in journal entries interspersed with dramatized scenes. He'd have been better off to pick one of those forms and stick with it. For one thing, the journal entries tend to rehash what we've already witnessed in the scenes. New story elements relayed in the journal sequences would have more impact on the reader if they were acted out. Every journal entry slows the pace of the story.

The author might make these entries work by paring them to the bone, stripping excess verbiage, and making certain each journal segment offers new story information. He also has to be careful these sequences don't repeat what we already know, unless that material is presented from a new perspective that offers fresh insights for the reader. These entries also must be vividly written, memorably phrased, and alive with strong images. Otherwise, slackened pace results in slackened interest for the reader and editor.

At another point in the same story, the author inserts a long monologue. One character who is a psychiatrist comments in detail on another character's behavior and life. This is a blatant example of an author telling when he should be showing. The effect is monotonous. By the time the revelations come, we've lost interest in both the commentator and the character being commented upon. To make matters worse, the revelations themselves are rather mundane.

We are bored first by the humdrum tone of the presentation, then by the humdrum nature of what is presented. This passage should have been: (1) Shortened drastically; (2) Reimagined for higher interest; (3) Written as a dialogue in an effectively dramatized scene of talk and action.

Still, none of the above affectations bother me as much as being pounded on the head with theme. I worry when an author tells me the theme of a book he hasn't written yet. This author is making the process of storytelling too intellectual, especially for popular fiction. A story needs to be more charmed and magical than that, as does the experience of writing it. Trust the theme to emerge from the story, never the other way around. A story written to illustrate a theme will tend to feel as if it was contrived by the author to serve his thematic priority. There is little chance of arriving at the emotional truth, the heart, of your story when you approach it primarily from the head. You rob yourself, and your reader, of the wondrous experience of discovery when you decide in advance what that discovery will be.

Finally, don't try to wow us by manipulating point of view just because you have the mistaken notion that manipulation will make your manuscript stand out from the rest. If you've taken my advice so far, you're well on your way to creating a fascinating and appealing protagonist. If you intend to craft a fascinating and appealing story as well, you will be best served by telling your story from the point of view of that person you worked so hard to create.

Your protagonist is the most interesting character in your story, the one who makes things happen, the one with the most involving way of seeing and doing. Who could possibly have a consciousness more likely to hook your reader and keep him hooked? Whether your protagonist narrates in the first or third person should be determined by the needs of the specific story. Just make sure the telling is done in the most compelling voice available to you. That is the surest way to stand out.

Secret #40: Ten Tips That Never Go Out of Style

1. It's all about the work. How many times have I told you the story is the thing? That's true as far as it goes. Beyond that, the quality of the work is the thing, and the work of a novel is the writing. Don't tell yourself that an author of great stories can get away with sloppy writing and amateurish style. That occasionally may have been true in the past, when publishers were putting out more titles and needed more books, but this is no longer the case.

Publisher lists shrink more every year, and as they do, editors get fussier. You must know your craft. My advice: If you're not taking a writing class or working with a mentor, now's the time to start. Never stop studying your craft, because you can never be perfect at it. In fact, you'll probably never be as good as you want to be, whether you know that or not. And, if you do notice a sloppy writer who is breaking newly into print, don't tell yourself you'll be the next one. Trust me. You won't be.

2. Every writer has her personal writing tics—mistakes she makes over and over again. She doesn't see them because they've become habitual, and she doesn't truly realize they're wrong. That's why it's difficult to identify your tics for yourself. This is where a reading partner, another author who reviews your work in return for your review of his, comes in handy. This person can become familiar with your writing style, including those quirks or tics, and will tend to spot them more readily than you would. Find yourself such a partner, either in person or online, and listen to what he says.

3. Beware of warm-up writing. This happens most often at beginnings—the beginning of the book, the beginning of a chapter, the beginning of a scene. The action is postponed for several pages while the writer natters on in preparation for writing that action. He is like a musician pecking at the keyboard, fingering out phrases that may suggest the main movement to come but that are not yet fully formed into that movement. Save your warm-ups for the gym. Get into the meat of the story right from the start.

4. Words are the tools of your craft. Use them carefully. Do not abuse them. Choose the word that most closely and clearly communicates what you want to say. Write with your thesaurus at your elbow, and

consult it continually. But once you've found that right word, don't belabor it. Do not repeat the word, or even a form of that word, in close proximity in your text. This is an error that is easier to spot on the page than on the computer screen. Never edit your work on screen. Always print it out and edit on hard copy. You will do a better job of finding and correcting errors that way.

5. Use adverbs and adjectives sparingly. Verbs are the appropriate part of speech tools for making your writing descriptive. Collect strong, expressive verbs. Make lists of them in your writer's journal. Copy them out of your thesaurus. Use them to give your writing power. Writing with too many adjectives and adverbs tends to be flabby and overwritten. Writing full of powerful verbs is taut and has impact.

6. Eradicate quirks of emphasis. Say you want the reader to place emphasis on a certain word or phrase to recognize its importance. Or you want a phrase to be read a certain way. So, you underline words or add exclamation points or capitalize at will or set off a phrase with dashes. All I can say is, "Don't do it!" That exclamation point is justified, because I want to make a very strong point here. These quirks of emphasis make your prose feel and sound as if it was written by a gushy adolescent. Unless that is the voice you are trying to achieve, don't do it.

7. Pay attention to paragraph length. Are your paragraphs too short? I recall one author who wrote long sentences and set each one off as a paragraph. The effect was choppy, both on the page and in the reading. Are your paragraphs too long—great gouts of words that go on and on for line after line? Quicken the pace of your writing by breaking your narrative into shorter paragraphs.

8. Use line breaks appropriately. A line break is a space between lines of text with a short, straight line across the center. This straight line is preceded and followed by an empty line. Every change of scene within a chapter—each switch from one time and place to another, or one unit of action to another—should be signaled by a line break. Do not use line breaks to indicate emphasis.

9. Pare down the fat in your writing. Mystery novelist Dick Francis tells of an editor from his newspaper days who would lean over his shoulder and ask, "Why is that word in there?" As a result, Francis writes some of the sparest—as in, least fatty—prose around. For an example of what I'm talking about, read his work, especially his descriptions. Accomplished writers are always our best teachers.

10. Finally, be assured that you are in charge of your story. You are the creator of the world of your book. Don't tell yourself you can't make changes to your story, as if it had been dictated to you from on high and must not be altered. When it comes to the elements of your story, you are the supreme being. You can and must make any change that will strengthen your story. Your story is fluid, not static. You alone decide where, and how smoothly, it will flow.

Crossroads

AN AUTHOR SELF-INTERROGATION

Choose a single, long scene from your manuscript. Remember what I said about being hard-nosed in judging the sophistication of your writing style. That is what you must be, as you read your chosen scene and ask yourself the following questions:

- How many adjectives and adverbs do you use in this scene? Underline each one. Then go back and ask yourself if each of them is necessary.
- How many "lovely passages" of lyrical writing have you included? Underline these passages. Reread each one and ask yourself if each is necessary.
- Is there at least one closely observed detail in each character description and each setting description? Ask yourself if each description is as sensual, visual, emotional, haunting, and original as it can be.
- Is there enough dialogue in your scene? At least half of the scene—up to 70 percent for popular fiction—should be dialogue.
- Is the dialogue exciting? Have you included small talk rather than making sure everything your characters say is significant to your story situation?
- Can you differentiate one speaker from another? Remove the dialogue tags that identify speakers, read the quotes out of order, and ask yourself if your reader would be able to identify each speaker from only what he says.
- Does your dialogue have subtext? What, if anything, is going on between the lines of what is being said? How does that complicate the story?
- Do you describe the dialogue? Underline every dialogue tag. Wherever you have used a phrase other than he said or she said, consider changing to these simpler, more preferable tags.
- Do you try to impress your reader with your intelligence and erudition? Underline every word that isn't generally heard in everyday speech. Underline every phrase that doesn't read as if it might be spoken by a contemporary human being in contemporary real-life. Underline any references to literary works or

academic sources, any foreign words or phrases, and anything else esoteric or quirky. Ask yourself why you have included these words and phrases. Do they really make your story more powerful, resonant, and clearly communicated?

- Is your writing spare and clean? Pretend you are Dick Francis's former newspaper editor, and ask yourself to justify every word and phrase you have used.
- Is your writing melodramatic? Underline every instance in which you use a word or phrase or manner of description for the purpose of evoking a particular emotional response from your reader. Ask yourself if you really need to do that.
- Is your writing stylish? Reread the ten tips in secret number forty. Ask yourself if, in this scene, you've taken each one to heart in your writing.

Review your honest and thorough responses to the above questions. Those responses more or less constitute an analysis of your fiction writing style and its strengths and its weaknesses. List those strengths and weaknesses in your writer's journal. Pledge to yourself that you will make the most of your strengths and minimize your weaknesses in your future writings.

Are You There Yet?

A HANDS-ON EXERCISE

Review the previous questions regarding style until their content and the concerns they raise are firmly established in your mind. While still in that consciousness, choose one of the following quotations and write the scene it inspires in your writer's journal.

- "It was eleven o'clock of a spring night in Florida. It was Sunday. Any other night she would have been in bed for two hours by this time." (from *Sweat*, by Zora Neale Hurston)
- "I was never a virgin. Okay, in the technical sense, of course I was." (from *Lily White*, by Susan Isaacs)
- "They sought one another's hands over the shoulders of the guests crowding around them." (from *Le Mariage*, by Diane Johnson)
- "All those times we tried to kill his little brother were just for fun." (from *Back Roads*, by Tawni O'Dell)
- "How could he talk to me that way? How could he? I didn't have to stick my neck out for him. I didn't have to do shit for him." (from *Mona in the Promised Land*, by Gish Jen)

Using those same questions and considerations from the Crossroads interrogation, analyze the writing style of your freshly written scene. Note in your writer's journal how this analysis differs from your previous analysis of the scene from your current work. Which of your strengths did you capitalize on in this new scene, and how? Which of your weaknesses did you minimize, and how?

Passage

ALL'S WELL THAT ENDS STUPENDOUSLY

The ending of your story is as important as the opening—maybe even more important, assuming you want the reader to invest in your next book. The ending is your last impression on the reader. Will that impression leave her eager for your next book or ready to throw this present one against the wall? If you hope to make a fan of the reader, and the editor, the ending must be strong rather than weak, riveting rather than dull, and organic to the story rather than contrived. After a reader has finished a book, she either will or will not talk about it. That talk usually happens when the reader has enjoyed the experience of the story all the way through, including the ending. Such talk is what we call word of mouth, and nothing means more to the success of a book and the future prospects of its author.

Secret #41: Concluding Clunkers

Unfortunately, maybe even unfairly, if the ending of your story doesn't leave the reader with a good feeling, that supportive word of mouth won't occur. No matter how well the rest of the story was received, no positive "buzz" will happen—not with the help of this reader, anyway. You must never forget that you build a writing career, along with a loyal audience for your work, one reader at a time. The authors of the following stories should have kept that in mind.

In my first example from my rejected manuscript pile, the author makes the mistake of shying away from the necessary confrontation in his concluding scenes. He starts out well, bringing us to the end of his story in fairly good order. The adversarial parties are poised to tangle. Everything that has happened to this point in the story—the protagonist's struggles, wins, and losses—is on the line. This is popular fiction, so we can assume the protagonist, Mitch, will prevail. Only the details of his triumph, and the manner in which those details will be presented, are in serious question.

Mitch's story climax takes too long to happen. The pacing is misguided. The confrontation begins in a blow-by-blow rhythm, but the author neglects to take us inside the emotions of the characters. Under such tense circumstances, the characters must be experiencing powerful feelings, but we have no direct proof of that. Instead, first one thing happens, then another and another, like the rat-a-tat of a machine gun. This relentless, unvaried rhythm distances us from the characters. We are never drawn into the intensity of the scene. The author makes the mistake of resorting to long passages of narrative, which deaden active scenes. This scene could be brought to life by replacing much of the narrative with closely observed details added carefully, without slowing the pace of the scene.

Mitch's story includes other action scenes prior to this one. Each of those previous scenes was more fully imagined, details and all, than this final pivotal encounter. Perhaps the author thought he was paring this confrontation scene down to the essentials to pace the finale more rapidly. If so, he went too far. He needs to reinvent this scene in a manner that allows the reader to savor the confrontation at the same time she is being swept up in it.

Our second example presents a different problem. Many stories involve mysteries to be solved, whether these stories are mystery novels or not. Whenever the question "What's going to happen next?" forms in a reader's mind, suspense is created. That question should form as close to the first line of the book as possible. A savvy author drafts her dramatic story opening to inspire both that question and the reader's need to know the answer. The author must feed that need throughout the story. Without it, the reader has no compulsion to turn pages all the way to the end.

The author of protagonist Judith's story neglects to take "all the way to the end" as seriously as she should. She answers the principal suspense question too soon. As in lots of stories, that question revolves around a bad guy—or gal. Who is this person causing so much trouble for the protagonist? If this were a mystery novel, that question would involve the identity of a murderer. But as I said before, "Whodunit?" as a central story question is not confined to the mystery genre.

What about Charles Dickens's *Great Expectations*? The central story question of this classic novel focuses on protagonist Pip's sudden, unexpected good fortune and what—or whom—its source may be. Dickens uses a timeworn genre staple, the red herring, to complicate Pip's mystery. Dickens misdirects our gaze, and Pip's, toward a possible answer that seems probable but turns out to be a blind alley.

Stories also can be built around questions other than "Whom?" Your mystery might be the "How?" of the situation causing the protagonist his trouble and conflict. Your story's "Why?" could zero in on a character's unknown motivation, or could focus more broadly on why this situation is happening in general. The narrative process of unraveling the answer to the central question of the story is, in essence, the plot of that story.

Therefore, it stands to reason that once the central question is answered, the plot is finished. The author of Judith's story reasons otherwise. She answers the central question well before the end of the book. The story dribbles on from there and, eventually, fades off the page, taking the reader's interest along with it.

By the way, Charles Dickens does the same thing, but he gets away with it. We learn the true identity of Pip's benefactor with a fair hunk of story left to go. But Dickens is a master storyteller. He has posed a second central story question, a favorite of many authors all on its own: "Will the boy and girl get together?" In this case, "Will Pip and Estella, an unlikely couple if there ever was one, get together?" And, "If they do get together, given how unsuited they are, how will this outcome seem like a probable one?" Dickens answers those questions as only a master can and, ironically, leaves his readers longing for more. The author of Judith's story should have pursued greater expectations of herself as a storyteller.

In our third flawed example, the author does keep us on tenterhooks until the last possible moment. We have absolutely no idea what the answer to the central story question might be or, in particular, how that solution could possibly come about. As it turns out, the author may have had no idea either. In the final climactic scene, no resolution is in sight. Our expectation is at fever pitch. We ask ourselves how this story is going to end. Suddenly, the protagonist's mail arrives. In that mail delivery, he finds an envelope with a computer-generated address label and no sender identification. An anonymous clipping inside provides the key to solving the story problem and answers the central story question.

In old-fashioned melodramas, this type of concluding device was called the deus ex machina. The solution to the story dilemma, in the form of some sort of miraculous intervention, was literally dropped from the sky or, occasionally, rose through a trap door from beneath the stage. The apparently insoluble problems of the players are brought to a swift and happy conclusion. The audience of that period, thoroughly steeped in notions of divine providence, readily accepted this device as plausible—or so we are told. Contemporary readers are hardly as tolerant.

The story solution, the answer to the central question, must be adequately prepared for. The conclusion, when it comes about, must feel natural and inevitable. We, as readers, respond with a combination of recognition and surprise. We also suspect we should have known the story would end this way all along. In this example, the arrival of the pivotal message at the eleventh hour is a contrivance. There is no natural outgrowth from the circumstances of the preceding chapters and, therefore, no inevitability.

The author saves herself the work of finding a more artful story solution. She might have set her protagonist about the task of discovering the information in that anonymous message for herself. The author could have made that quest a source of trouble and conflict for the protagonist, further complicating the story and thickening the plot. The effort would surely have proven worthwhile for both author and reader, yielding a stronger story and a credible ending. As written, the solution comes too easily for the protagonist and is, conversely, difficult for a reader or an editor to accept.

Equally lacking in plot foundation is the protagonist who performs a sudden, spontaneous action that leads to solving the story's problem. He takes a totally different direction from anything he's previously done, causing the story to turn out the way the author's plot plan requires. In the case of my next example, the protagonist suddenly makes a decision that is critical to the outcome of the story. We have no idea why he makes this decision. There is no motivation for it in the present scene or any previous scene, other than the motivation to extricate the poor protagonist from the quagmire his author has dumped him into and portray him as triumphant.

In the story of a similar protagonist, Robert, jumps to a conclusion that instantly solves the conundrum of the story. The conclusion he comes to leaps over a chasm between the knowledge he possessed up to this moment and the knowledge that occurs to him in an alleged flash of brilliance. Robert is a smart guy, but we have a hard time believing he's this smart. We have difficulty because there is no motivation for his brainstorm, no chain of discovery leading logically to this moment of illumination.

Again, these discoveries could have been hard-won via admirable struggles by the protagonist in the face of formidable obstacles. That would have made Robert's story a stronger one. Instead, this author also opts for the easy way out. He avoids the true work, and the joy, of storytelling: to weave a tale that builds into a cohesive whole through all of its strands. So woven, a story holds together because each plot turn is well founded upon previous turns and because each character action is well grounded in strong and established motives, especially at the story's end.

Lack of motivation is just as devastating to a story, sometimes even more devastating, when the antagonist's behavior is the problem. This character has caused a lot of trouble for the protagonist, and for others as well. Often the identity of this troublemaking antagonist is withheld until the end of the story, though that is not always the case. In many stories, especially suspense thrillers, we learn the antagonist's identity early on so we can see how dangerous he is, how potentially lethal he is to the protagonist we've come to care about and admire.

Revelation of the antagonist's identity, whenever it may occur, is crucial to story success. That antagonist's motivations are equally crucial. If we don't believe that this character could have done such dastardly things for these reasons, the story fails. Specifically, the ending of the story fails. That is what happens to this next example story.

This is a murder mystery with several heinous killings; an old woman, a young girl, and several others are brutally murdered. The culprit turns out to be the old woman's son and the young girl's supposed friend. Why did he do it? We don't know. We need to understand. We don't need to empathize with the killer and his motives, but we do need to understand why he did it, particularly with crimes as bloodthirsty as the ones in this story. Unfortunately, we are never in the mind of this killer. Therefore, we are never privy to this motivation, and that is a huge storytelling mistake.

My suggestion: Insert a single passage in the final confrontation scene, a passage from the killer's point of view. As the killer waits and watches, fragments of his brutal history flash through his mind, and each fragment contains a piece of his reason for what he's done. These flashes must not go on too long, or the forward momentum of the story will be lost. Consequently, the passage is brief, but by the end of it we understand what we need to understand about this character and his behavior. Of course, his motives must be compelling, at least as he sees them, for readers to accept these motives as credible.

Strength of motivation is the hinge upon which an effective story ending hangs. That goes for both the villain's motivations and the hero's. In a mystery novel in particular, the two questions that keep a reader turning pages are: Whodunit? and Why? The author must answer each of these questions thoroughly and satisfactorily for the ending of the story to succeed. Regardless of genre, if the ending does not succeed, the story as a whole falls short as well.

Secret #42: The Big Bang

In the popular arena, nearly nothing is accomplished by genteel means. Attracting mass attention is the object, and you don't do that with a bell and a whistle. You do it with a clang and a boom. In storytelling, that translates into drama and the large effect. Many pages ago, I advised you not to meander into your story. Similarly, I advise that you must not dribble out of your story. Drama and a large effect—a big bang—are required.

Always think of your story ending as it will be acted out in a concrete scene. Never focus on the abstract thematic impression you wish to leave behind. This doesn't mean there can't or won't be a theme in your work. It simply means you shouldn't be thinking about that theme or self-consciously directing your story toward it. Your priority must be to tell the story in a way that keeps lots of readers rapidly turning pages all the way to the very last one.

The scene's the thing. Action and dialogue are happening. Your ending, to have optimum impact, must be shown as it is taking place. Do not tell the reader about it from a distance. The point of view character must be at the center of this climactic event, in the heartbeat of the story at its most decisive moment. Otherwise, how can that narrating voice take your reader there as well? Observation of what goes on is at a safe remove. Immersion is what you must strive to achieve, and is anything but safe.

The protagonist and reader teeter together at the precipice, their nerves jangling, their respiration altered. Will they topple or triumph? That is the central story question now. All other considerations pale. Everything depends upon the outcome. This is the level of tension and the tone that you must create. Polite half-measures will not do. You cannot be merely close to the focus of the action; you are in the action. The purpose of the big bang ending is to reverberate after the last page turns, to lodge in the psyche of the reader and be remembered, all the way to the bookstore to purchase your next title.

You must plan the climactic scene in detail. Don't write a word of your final scene until you devise the perfect plan for the resulting scene to have a big bang impact.

- Plan mostly action and dialogue, using very little narrative.
- Plan to keep all of this action on stage, in the immediate present.
- Plan dialogue that is spare, to the point, and memorable.
- Plan on intensifying the pace, making it faster than before.
- Plan lots of physical movement in the scene.
- Plan lots of sound, smell, texture, and other intense sensations.
- Plan to plunge your protagonist into peril, and to worsen it.
- Plan one more formidable obstacle to arise for your protagonist.
- Plan a confrontation between your protagonist and antagonist.
- Plan on milking the confrontation while keeping the intense pace.
- Plan for your protagonist to cause action, not merely be overtaken by it.
- Plan to communicate your protagonist's feelings, with impact, to the reader.
- Plan to incorporate fear, even terror, among those emotions.
- Plan the presence of real danger to your protagonist.
- Plan an outcome in the balance.
- Plan that outcome as crucial to your protagonist.
- Plan for your protagonist to be nearly vanquished.

- Plan for your protagonist to be racing against time.
- Plan for your protagonist to triumph at the last moment.
- Plan for your protagonist to triumph by the narrowest margin.
- Plan for this triumph to be uplifting and inspiring.
- Plan all of the above step-by-step, as a choreographer plans a dance.

Work the scene out in this manner, and you will create a powerful climax for your story—a big bang dramatic ending that comes full circle from your dramatic opening. Afterward, your job is to recognize that your story is over. You and your protagonist have exploded out of the explosive situation you exploded into on page one. You absolutely must resist the temptation to hang around any longer. You've taken your reader on an unforgettable ride. Leave before she has a chance to catch her breath. Leave her wanting more.

End with a maximum of only one and a half pages of denouement, concluding comments, or summaries. Do you hear me shouting at you? "One and a half pages max!" No exceptions. Go back and tie up loose story ends, details that require closure from earlier on, but don't tie them up in this page and a half at the end. That would give them too much significance. Eke out these minor endnotes, one at a time, throughout the final two chapters of the story. But in these very last pages, break clean quickly.

You're left with just one more thing to do: Craft a closing line at least as memorable as the opening line you crafted way back at the beginning of your story. Make this line a jewel, painstakingly selected for its brilliance, masterfully cut, and polished until every facet gleams. Make it short, direct, declarative, and decisive. Make it ring in the consciousness of your readers as unforgettably as, "My dear, I don't give a damn," or "After all, tomorrow is another day."

Secret #43: Satisfaction

We have to do some thinking now about feelings. I've talked a lot about focusing on your characters' feelings, on identifying what is going on inside them, and on bringing that emotional truth alive on the page. I've also talked about the purpose of all of this being to duplicate those feelings inside the reader and, by doing so, commit the reader emotionally to your story. Now the story has ended. What should the feelings be?

What do you want your reader to be feeling when she reads the final line, leaves the final page, and puts the book down? You want her to be satisfied. This means you want her to believe wholeheartedly that your story was worth the time and emotional commitment she made to it.

How do you make sure your reader is satisfied with the experience of reading your story? First and foremost, you follow the advice from this book for creating your characters and crafting your plot. Then you write an ending that lives up to the reader expectations you've created via these deep characters in this intense story.

I have discussed the components of a successful ending previously in this passage. Here are some further considerations related specifically to writing a satisfying ending:

• **Consider the audience you are seeking to satisfy.** If you are writing a literary novel, you are, generally, very free in your ending options. Your story resolution may be ambiguous, with little or nothing resolved. The characters, and the reader, are left up in the air. This is, of course, an unsettling experience, but readers of literary fiction are accustomed to being unsettled. They may even be seeking that experience. In fact, the protagonist can fail altogether in a literary novel, with the reader disillusioned about the story situation and life in general as a result. The only real rule in this kind of writing is that the ending must conform to the author's vision of the story.

In popular fiction, the parameters of a satisfying ending are much more restrictive than in literary fiction. I've mentioned the triumph of the protagonist previously in this passage. You've created a strong protagonist who is decent, decisive, active, and generally admirable. You have inspired the reader to care about this character. In a sense, you have manipulated the reader into doing so. Do you think your reader will be satisfied if you now drag that protagonist he cares about down to defeat? I think not.

• **Consider your audience's expectations.** In popular fiction, the ending must be conclusive. Little of the ambiguity permitted in literary fiction is permissible here. The reader wants to know exactly what's what, particularly with the protagonist. How has this situation been resolved for her? What will her reality be, vis-à-vis this story situation, after the last page of this book has been turned? From the beginning to the end of this story, a change has been wrought, especially upon the protagonist. A circle that began on page one is now closed. These are not arbitrary circumstances. They are concrete, defined, and visible, and that is satisfying for the reader. He can heave a sigh of relief. All has ended well for the protagonist. If there is any room for the arbitrary here, it is in the fates of the secondary characters. One of these, most effectively a prominent character, can suffer an ambiguous or even tragic ending. This even can enhance the protagonist's triumph by contrasting with it.

• **Remember your ending is the last impression your protagonist will make on the reader.** This impression is made most pointedly in the climactic scene. Entangle your reader's emotions even more inextricably with the fate of your protagonist by causing her to struggle valiantly in this scene against great odds and obstacles—and be nearly defeated. Her well-being, perhaps her life, hangs in the balance. Defeat looms closer and closer. Then, in the nick of time, she triumphs by being the best, strongest, boldest, smartest, and most courageous she can possibly be. Not only has she won, she also has proven herself, despite truly formidable odds against her. She is, in fact, the heroine the reader always believed her to be. The reader feels the additional satisfaction of being vindicated in his judgment, of having backed the right team in the conflict of this story situation.

Your hero should never turn out to be the villain of your story. If you have created a protagonist readers care about and admire, how do you think they will feel if that character turns out to be the perpetrator of bad or even evil deeds? The answer is obvious. There are rare stories in which an author can violate this dictum and still leave the reader satisfied with the ending. You pose yourself a difficult challenge if you make this choice. I advise against doing so, particularly with your early stories, if you hope to satisfy readers and, more immediately, attract an editor to your work.

• **Consider the contemporary mindset.** A word, or several words, about the female protagonist: It used to be the case that the hero, the male protagonist, was expected to step in and save the heroine from peril at the end of the story. That is no longer the expectation. The heroine is expected to save herself, especially in the popular fiction novel directed toward a female readership. A strong protagonist does not need to be rescued. She may not have as much physical strength as a man, but she has mental, spiritual, and moral strength. She will rely on these to bring about her own triumph. The female reader will feel pleased and, yet again, vindicated by this conclusion. In some stories, the heroine may even save the hero. Another option is that the hero may assist the heroine in this confrontation scene. They struggle together as a team. They are nearly vanquished together, and together they triumph. This is a particularly effective ending for a story where the heroine and hero are romantically involved and the reader hopes for them to be together after the story ends.

• **Consider the fate of your antagonist.** This is what I call comeuppance time. Just as the reader feels satisfied and vindicated by your protagonist's triumph, your reader will feel satisfied and vindicated by your antagonist's defeat. Again, I remind you that we are concerned with fulfilling the expectations of the popular fiction reader. At the satisfying ending of such a novel, good wins and bad loses. By the same token, retribution follows defeat. There must be promise, if not on-the-page imposition, of just punishment for the misdeeds of the story villain. The specifics and the severity of that punishment should be commensurate with the specifics and the severity of the villain's misdeeds. Commercially successful exceptions—for example, *Presumed Innocent* by Scott Turow—are few enough to prove the rule. Although, even in this case, you might consider the possibility that the antagonist suffers inwardly and spiritually for what she has done and will be haunted by it for the rest of her life. What if your villain is simply a sociopath without conscience? This is sticky territory where reader satisfaction is concerned. Again, I advise against toying with such ambivalence, especially in your early work.

• **Consider the passive ending.** This is a classic of some classic mystery authors. Agatha Christie is a prime example. She ends many of her novels with a parlor explanation scene. One of her sleuth protagonists—Hercule Poirot or Miss Marple or whoever—gathers all of the story principals, including the suspects, in a parlor or some similar venue and explains to them, and to us, what has happened in the story. The sleuth runs us through the workings of his mind—how the murder happened, his steps in searching out the murderer, who that murderer might be, and the specifics of the motive. This may be okay with Christie fans, but I think of it as a good bad example of the author telling what she should be showing.

The same principle holds true of final confrontations in which the villain gets the upper hand and uses that opportunity to brag about his nefarious accomplishments, thus clarifying his actions and motives. This is a tough device to make original, since it has been resorted to so many times. Even worse is the spontaneous confession, where the adversary simply admits her guilt and blurts out her reasons for what she did. Where is the satisfaction of confrontation, the struggle against terrible odds, the fate in the balance, and the hard-won victory in any of these scenarios?

• **Consider the false ending.** This is a favorite of some thriller filmmakers. Brian De Palma comes to mind. The primary conflict situation in the story is resolved, and the sole villain is unmasked, or so we think. But there is another danger, a more subtle, more sinister threat yet to be confronted. The storytelling advantage here is that the protagonist is no longer alert, and her support systems, believing the danger to have passed, have usually retired from the scene. Dramatic irony is intensified to ultimate pitch as we, the audience, see this new and more potent danger, even though the protagonist does not. We long to leap onto the page and warn this character. Our frustration at not being able to shout such a warning and be heard maximizes our emotional involvement in the story. Then, the second confrontation, the most perilous one for the protagonist, is upon us. Imagine our satisfaction when this conflict squeaks to a nick-of-time triumph for the protagonist. That is a high degree of satisfaction indeed.

• **Consider popular genre expectations.** You have, I hope, satisfied reader expectations of your popular fiction characters by having them behave, at the end, in ways their previous story actions proved them capable of. You have, I hope, satisfied reader expectations of your plot by having the ending come as a surprise but not as an improbability. Your reader has been subtly prepared, by both character and plot, for what happens in the climactic scene. These behaviors and events strike your reader as logical in terms of previous behaviors and events. Your reader thinks, "Of course! I should have seen that coming."

Having accomplished the above, are you also certain you have satisfied reader expectations of the specific genre category you are writing in? If you are writing mystery or suspense, has the offense of the antagonist turned out to be as heinous as originally portrayed? Was this, in fact, a murder story after all? It had better be. Don't have the death turn out to be a suicide or an accident. There is much less satisfaction there because there is no antagonist other than the victim himself. Consequently, no fitting retribution occurs. Reader satisfaction is diminished significantly, and an established convention of the genre has been ignored.

Similarly, with a romance novel, the hero and heroine must get together in the end for reader (and editor) satisfaction to occur. In other words, a reader comes to these genres, and others, assuming that certain basic ground rules will be adhered to. These ground rules vary with each genre category. You must find out what they are for your genre of choice. Otherwise, you are in peril of seriously disappointing reader expectations, and that is not a wise thing for an author, at any stage of her career, to do.

Secret #44: Volunteer for the Drafts

Veteran best-selling popular fiction author Phyllis A. Whitney says, "When you accept the fact that revision is a necessary part of successful writing, you will be able to face it professionally."

THE FACTS OF MANUSCRIPT REVISION

Fact One: It is preferable that you complete the first draft of your novel before beginning the revision process. During your writing of that first draft, don't make judgments or edit yourself. Write as close to a white-hot pace as possible all the way through. Only then will you have a full canvas to work on, a complete story to rethink and rework. Only then will you be totally convinced that you do in fact have a novel here, a complex enough story to constitute a book. Only then will you feel the satisfaction of having committed your story to paper, in your own words, from your own imagination, according to your own vision. This is a crucial accomplishment for a writer. There are, of course, other ways of writing a novel. This is simply the one that works best in my experience, from my own writing career as well as the careers of authors I have worked with.

Fact Two: The one possible exception to the above involves the first chapter of your story. The dramatic opening must hook the editor's and the reader's attention, so it has great significance. This, on its own, does not necessitate immediate revision. However, the first chapter also establishes the essential elements of your story: the tone, the mood, the situation, the personalities of the main characters, and probably their motivations as well. These elements constitute the foundation of your story. If that foundation is not securely constructed, the rest will be on shaky ground and likely to flounder. With this in mind, I allow for the possibility of stopping to revise that vital first chapter before venturing onward—but do so in absolutely no more than three drafts, including the first one, please.

Fact Three: A positive attitude toward revision is essential to becoming a professional writer. Revision is the part of the process where the raw material of your story elements is refined into the finished product. Too many authors think of revision as a chore and approach it grudgingly. These are authors foolish enough to send their manuscripts to editors and agents after only the first draft has been written. These are authors almost certain to be rejected. You must think of the revision process as an opportunity to do your very best work. You also must think of the revision process as a creative experience, as creative as writing the first draft. In revision, your characterizations take on further depth, your plot develops subtext, your dialogue sparkles with new wit, and your details are observed more closely. I liken the writing of a first draft to running along the surface of your story, recording its events and interactions as you observe them happening in your imagination. In subsequent drafts, you stop at various points on that surface and delve deeper—into character, scene detail, action. This is where the richness of a story comes to life. The author, freed from the momentum of getting the story down on paper, takes his time to discover story layers and elements previously unrevealed. During the revision process, the good story can become exceptional. Adjust your attitude toward revision to take that possibility into account.

Fact Four: It is best to put the novel away for a while after you complete the first draft. Do not begin revising right away. Take a vacation from the story, albeit a brief one. Do other things not related to this story. If ideas for the revision come to you, record them briefly in some accessible form—note cards, a small notebook, or a file folder—then forget about them until your hiatus is finished. Don't take off such a long period of time that the story goes cold inside you. Just take long enough to get out of that intense attachment you feel to the first draft after just finishing it. You will need more objectivity than that to revise your story successfully.

Fact Five: An outside editor can sometimes help at this point, but it is up to you. If you'd like to try, hire a professional editor for a reasonable fee established in writing upfront. Tell the editor that you are about to commence with your second draft, or with whatever draft this may be. You want suggestions for how to strengthen and improve what you've written so far. Don't misinterpret this editing as a guarantee of acceptance. Check your editor's references to verify her expertise, especially with the type of book you are writing. Be confident that this person can actually help your work become more marketable. Don't hire an outside editor until you feel this confidence in her.

Fact Six: Realize that most publishing house editors do more acquisition than editing. Your manuscript must be the absolute best you can do when it first arrives on the editor's desk. Do not expect that an editor or a literary agent will see through the flawed execution of your story to what you consider the perfection of your talent underneath. He will not do that. He is not interested in doing that. You must eliminate flaws before you submit to anyone.

Fact Seven: Take whatever time is required for revising your manuscript before you submit. The object is not to write fast and submit faster. The object is to write the best novel you have in you and submit when it has achieved that level of excellence, not before. Be patient. You will not hurry your career along by rushing a manuscript into submission. Instead, rushing yourself could sabotage your career and squander your chances of a favorable editorial read.

Fact Eight: Cutting your own words can feel like pulling hairs out of your nostrils. You must get over those feelings right now, or you will never be a successful professional writer. Develop distance from your words. Think of them as separate from yourself and show them no mercy. What doesn't strengthen your story has to go.

Fact Nine: Adding material can be just as tough. Examine your story with an unforgiving eye to determine where it needs fleshing out, further dialogue, more scene description, or added subtext. An outside reader, someone who knows your work and can be objective, might help you with this. Ask this reader to note instances that need to provide something more for the reader to understand and experience the story fully. Choose someone you trust implicitly for this task. Then use your own writerly instinct to determine which suggestions you will incorporate into your story.

Fact Ten: The specifics of what you should be revising can be found in the previous passages of this book. Character development, plot structure, attention to detail, dialogue, style points, and other elements are all covered here. Before beginning your revision, review those passages. This review should provide you with the pointers you need to polish your manuscript until it is the strongest submission you have in you at this time in your writing life.

The best preparation for the revision phase, and all other phases, of your writing is to learn the writer's craft. An important step in that learning process is to build a writer's library. If you've not begun such a library, you must do so now. These are books that you buy and own, read and annotate, keep on a shelf, and refer to again and again. I offer you some suggestions from my own library. This is only a partial listing of the scores of volumes I own on the subjects of writing and publishing. Please, add titles of your own.

The Elements of Style by Strunk and White—the latest edition.
Bird by Bird by Anne Lamott—what it feels like to be a writer.
The Art of Fiction by John Gardner—a very dense instruction manual.
Story by Robert McKee—a very specific storytelling technique.
The Forest for the Trees: An Editor's Advice to Writers by Betsy Lerner.
Writing in Restaurants by David Mamet—lots about storytelling by a major playwright.
Beyond Style: Mastering the Finer Points of Writing by Gary Provost.
Make Your Words Work: Proven Techniques for Effective Writing by Gary Provost.
Follow the Story by James B. Stewart—storytelling, even in nonfiction.
Elements of Storytelling: How to Write Compelling Fiction by Peter Rubie.
Writing the Blockbuster Novel by Albert Zuckerman.
Writing the Breakout Novel by Donald Maas.
(The last three titles were written by literary agents who know the writing craft—and the writing business—inside out.)

Secret #45: Please, Please the Editor

One of the hardest things to handle in a writing career is criticism of your work. Most of us have experienced that before submitting to editors and agents. We give our work to our critique groups, writing partners, friendly readers, and spouses. We think that prepares us for criticism from the real authority of the publishing world. It does not.

Let me revise my opening statement. One of the hardest things to handle in a writing career is your work being criticized by book editors and literary agents. Nothing raises defenses, and hackles, as fast as that kind of criticism. You want to explain what this distant outsider obviously has not understood about your work. Blood pressure mounts, heart pounds, you can't wait to get your word in. "Yes, but . . ." you begin. You need to learn right now that this way of reacting to professional criticism shouts Amateur with a capitol A.

When this criticism happens verbally, by telephone or in person, keep calm and be silent. Bite your tongue through if you have to. Meanwhile, keep busy taking notes. Write down everything that is said to you. When the commentary is finished, thank this professional for her input and drop it at that. Say good-bye politely and hang up the phone, or change the subject if this is a face-to-face contact. Pocket the notes, and whatever your emotional reactions may be, until you are on your own. Feel free to mouth your objections, and your epithets, then.

That is the external control mechanism for responding to criticism. It involves your personal attitude toward your work. You have to learn a few basic truths right now:

1. There will be editors and agents who criticize and reject your work.
2. You must not take this personally. It may feel personal, but it isn't.

3. Editors and agents criticize and reject manuscripts for business reasons.

4. You must distance yourself and your reactions from these criticisms and rejections.

5. Create that distance by realizing your work is what you do. It isn't who you are.

Accept and internalize these truths, and you will have taken the first giant step toward learning to react to criticism as a professional rather than as an amateur. In the next step, you will learn to use that criticism appropriately—for the betterment of your work. Professional criticism from someone with daily and in-depth knowledge of the publishing business is a gift. It won't come to you often in the early stages of your submitting experience. When it does happen, be grateful.

Most of the time, you will receive a "Thanks, but no thanks" form letter in response to your manuscript submissions. Any personal communication is manna from heaven. Remember that this is a voice from the other side of the desk, a message from a publishing business professional about how to make your work more acceptable to that world. Take that message seriously. Study it. Learn everything you can from it. Then, revise your work accordingly. That's what a writing pro would do.

Most publishing professional criticism will come to you in written, rather than verbal form. That form, if you're lucky, will be a revision letter. Revision letters not only offer criticism and revision suggestions for your work, but they also request that you implement those suggestions and resubmit the result. That is the greatest gift of all. An editor or a literary agent found your work of enough interest to take the time to read a sizable portion of it, write down his responses, and send them off to you. He is also willing to read a revised version of your manuscript. This is your lucky day.

Believe it or not, lots of authors don't take such a request seriously. Or maybe they are offended by the notion that their work might need revision. In either case, they file the letter away, or destroy it, and ignore the request for resubmission. I had this happen to me numerous times in my editor/agent years. I've had authors tell me they thought I was just being polite. Take my word on this: When it comes to allocating precious, heavily encumbered time to reading yet another manuscript submission, editors and agents are not polite. We do not invite resubmissions unless we honestly are interested in the author and the work.

There are two stages at which an author might receive a revision request letter. First, you might receive a revision letter after an initial submission, either via an agent or on your own. There is no contract or contract offer involved at this stage. The editor or agent is simply making clear that she found enough promise in your work to want to see if you can make it conform more closely to her needs. As I said, consider this a very favorable sign. Now, to the best of your ability, do exactly what she says.

You may, on the other hand, examine her revision suggestions and reject them as irrelevant or misguided or both. In that case, just forget about this editor and resubmitting to her. Do not make the mistake of communicating your objections to her. She doesn't care, and you will jaundice her attitude toward you for subsequent submissions, as well. If you think your objections, your inferences that she doesn't know what she's talking about, will impress her with your astuteness, you could hardly be farther off base.

If, instead, you decide to follow this editor's advice and revise your work according to her suggestions, you have proven that you understand a basic tenet of the commercial fiction business. The editor or literary agent is just about always right. You will do your career the most good by going along with her view of what could make your work acceptable for her publishing house or agency. This is true because, at these initial stages, you have no clout on your side. All you have is your work's potential to sell and your own potential to be pleasant to work with.

The other stage at which you might receive a revision request letter is after a contract has been negotiated and agreed upon, meaning this editor's publishing house intends to print and release your novel. That contract does not preclude further revision of the manuscript. In fact, your early manuscripts almost always will require revision. In my opinion, that is yet another gift.

Personally, I would rather have my editor ask for revisions than not. I welcome the feedback from another imagination, another intelligence, especially that of someone with insight into the current publishing marketplace and what is selling there. In that way, I feel like I have a partner in the process of making my work as readable and as marketable as possible. I welcome that partnership and do my best to cooperate.

Almost never, in many years of editing and agenting experience, did I come across an editor with anything other than businesslike motivations for his criticisms of author submissions. Even criticism that might, to a sensitive author, seem excessive is more likely simply thoroughgoing, and that is yet another gift. Editors and agents don't offer criticism to be unkind or destructive. They are just doing their jobs, and giving you a leg up in your writing career.

By the same token, an absence of revision suggestions, though it may feel good to the ego, is not necessarily the best thing for the book, or for you as a writer with hopes of a long and successful career. Better to receive these criticisms before publication than after, when thumbs downs from readers and literary critics can threaten reception of your next book as well as this one.

I advise responding to a revision request after you've signed a contract in the same manner I've suggested responding to a one before the contract. Just say thank you. Then get to work collaborating with your editor or literary agent to make this the strongest story you've ever written.

The first and best reason for doing this is the last one I will mention. The competition is fierce out there, fiercer than it has ever been. These days, that is true for published authors as well as unpublished ones. Option books—additional titles submitted to fulfill the option clause in a previous contract—are being turned down with increasing regularity. For unpublished authors, unsolicited manuscripts submitted directly to an editor by an author, rather than via an agent, are just about universally rejected. Agented manuscripts by unpublished authors fare almost as badly with editors.

Which means you absolutely must get your book absolutely right. Train your psyche to work for you rather than against you at these final phases of writing your story—stop hating revision and start loving it. And welcome, even give joyous thanks for, any professional help that is mercifully offered to you.

Crossroads

AN AUTHOR SELF-INTERROGATION

Michael Ondaatje, author of *The English Patient*, says, "In all my books there is a discovery of story. You are unearthing and learning."

He's talking about digging for the emotional truth, the underneath of a story. At the end of writing your first draft, before continuing with subsequent polishes toward the final version, undertake a deep revision of your work by exploring the following questions:

- What is really going on here in the individual scenes? In the story as a whole? Don't just explore what the characters say is going on, or what they indicate on the surface is going on, or even what they think is going on. What do you, as creator of the universe of this story, know is going on? Keep in mind that some of this knowledge may still be hidden in the secrets your story universe has not yet revealed, even to you.

- What are the secrets here? What are your secrets, those parts of the story you have not yet excavated from the depths of your imagination? Keep in mind that these secrets underlie the text or surface of your story and are usually more true than that text or surface. These truths often exist despite what that text may have led you to believe is happening here.

- What are your characters' experiences really like? How do they feel, at the deep underneath heart level? What is it really like to be seduced? What is it really like to lose someone? What is it really like to fall in love? What is it really like to fear for your life? What is it really like to go through whatever your characters go through?

- Is your protagonist also an archeologist digging for the hidden truth of your story situation? How does your protagonist go about that search? Is your antagonist struggling to keep that truth hidden? How does your antagonist go about that struggle?

- What is revealed about the searcher, the digger, the questioner in this process of excavating for the truth? What does this character discover about himself? What do you, as author, discover about the inner truth of this character?

- What choices does this character make as a result of what he discovers in this story excavation process? What do these choices reveal about the inner truth of this character?

- What does this character feel as this search is pursued? What is his emotional truth? How does he act on these feelings? What do these actions reveal about his inner truth?

Are You There Yet?

A HANDS-ON EXERCISE

THE GET AND KEEP AN EDITOR EXERCISE

- Check your us-versus-them attitude at the door. Resentment of authority, coupled with any negatives you may have heard about the publishing business, can foster preconceptions in your mind, causing you to begin your author-editor relationship with both feet in a hole. Approach each editor with an open mind.

- On the other hand, resolve to be a warrior on behalf of your work and your career—a diplomatic warrior.

- Accept the fact that, for in-house editors, selection and acquisition of work for publication are business choices. Don't take rejections personally.

- How much do you need and want a positive relationship with your editor? Answer these questions: Do I need and want input from a publishing professional who can help me make my work stronger and more appealing to readers? Do I need and want an enthusiastic advocate for my work and my career within the system of a publishing house? Do I need and want an enthusiastic advocate who knows how to navigate the business better than I do?

- Begin your search for the best editor for your work with some hands-on, practical research. Go to the bookstore and find books and stories similar to your own. Check the acknowledgments pages of these books. A savvy author will have acknowledged and thanked his editor. From these sources, compile a list of editors who have acquired at least one book similar to your own for their publishing houses. List the publisher of each book along with the editor's name.

- Continue your research by accessing any source you can in reference to each individual editor: *Literary Market Place* listings, Internet mentions, databases of publishing publications (such as *Publishers Weekly*), and *Writer's Market*. Word of mouth also can be helpful, as long as you use your common sense and good judgment to evaluate what you hear. Keep in mind that you are looking for useful information about what each editor does and does not like in a manuscript. In other words, what kind of books with what specific elements does she prefer to acquire and publish?

- Attend writers' conferences and other events where editors appear in person. Watch for clues to what each editor is like personally—abrupt or slow, loquacious or reticent, etc. Be sober and objective in these judgments; they could prove crucial if you ever end up working with that editor. Most important, take every opportunity that may arise to listen to this editor, from attending panel discussions in which he participates to eavesdropping on his conversations at receptions and other gatherings. Note which authors this editor works with and publishes, especially if any of those authors are present at the conference or event. Create, if you can, the opportunity to speak to these authors. Ask discreetly about the author's experience with the editor and how that editor works.

- Keep a file of your research on these editors as you add them to your editorial possibilities list. Include everything you find out about each editor on your list in your file.

- Go to the Web site of each editor's publishing house. Explore the site for any mention of this particular editor, as well as for any information about books on this publisher's list that are similar to your own.

- If you determine that your work is ready for submission, prepare a professional submission package. Consult the Dos and Don'ts of the Being a Pro section of the next passage for preparation guidelines.

- Consult your preferred editor list. Before you submit your work, do research to find out if each of these publishing houses accepts simultaneous submissions (in which the manuscript is permitted to be sent out to several houses at once). Also check to see if they accept unsolicited (unagented) submissions. This information can be obtained from such sources as *Writer's Market* and individual publisher Web sites. As a last resort, call the publishing house and ask whoever answers the phone (there is no need to ask to speak with the editor to whom you are submitting).

- Submit your package simultaneously to several (six is optimum, in my opinion) publishing houses, as long as they accept simultaneous, unsolicited submissions.

- Make follow-up contact either two months later, with a respectful letter; or one month later, with a respectful e-mail (you can generally figure out each company's general e-mail formula for individual employees from its Web site). Subsequent attempts at contact should be equally respectful and should be conducted via e-mail. Do not telephone the editor; you defeat your purpose by incurring editor enmity that way. Throughout this process, you must be relentlessly pleasant and diplomatic, no matter how impatient, frustrated, or even exasperated you are feeling. Never let any of that show. Who knows? That strategy may get your manuscript read more quickly than would otherwise have been the case.

- Expect to be rejected. That is the norm. Consider this the audition process. You have to try out lots of times before landing a part. Do your best not to take it personally. Send a gracious thank you note to the editor for his attention (another savvy strategy). If he asked to see something else you've written, send it to him, by all means. But only send it once it is in strong, truly submittable form.

- Persist until you prevail. By prevail, I mean you get a call from an editor with a contract offer. By that point, you should have performed the next chapter's "get an agent" exercise and be set to obtain professional representation through the contract negotiation process.

- Good luck.

Passage 10

IT'S NOT OVER TILL YOU PUT IT OVER

Have you ever observed an actor selecting an audition piece—not only performing it, but selecting it, as well? He does so with great care, because he knows you never get a second chance to make a first impression. He has to walk into that audition and wow 'em from word one. You, as a submitting author, must do exactly the same thing. Think of presenting your work—to an agent, to an editor and to a potential reader—as an audition. Craft the tools of that presentation—your manuscript synopsis, your cover letter pitch and your promotional materials—as carefully as an actor selects and prepares the material that will earn her either a part in a play or a hook off the stage. Meanwhile, whether the verdict is thumbs-up or thumbs-down, he must always be professional. You, the author in search of a publisher, must do the same.

Secret #46: A Sin-Free Synopsis

Any fiction submission, including a complete manuscript, must be accompanied by a synopsis. That synopsis is a narrative summary of the main action of your story from beginning to end—not a summary of the sample chapters you may be sending as part of your submission, but a summary of your complete story all the way through. Synopsis lengths vary. I've heard a lot of editors ask for a two-page synopsis, but I wouldn't advise it. It is nearly impossible to communicate the depth and richness of a book-length story in two pages. Six pages is more realistic, in my opinion, but I wouldn't recommend going much longer than that. If your synopsis runs twelve, fifteen, twenty pages, you're telling too much. Remember, you're telling the *main* action of the story, nothing more.

It is crucial that you develop a talent for synopsis writing. The synopsis is the accepted and expected vehicle for showcasing your story, and your writing ability, to both editors and literary agents. Your synopsis must be composed as painstakingly as your book has been written. Otherwise, you shortchange your story and give it less than the polished, professional entrée it deserves. Too many writers dash off the synopsis as an afterthought. I caution you against doing that. Understand how important this particular process is. Undertake it accordingly.

Craft your synopsis. Polish it. Perfect it until it is your very best work. Think of synopsis writing as telling your story in the tradition of the ancient tribal storyteller who had to keep his audience hanging on every word or be banished into the wilderness with no supper. The stakes are equally high for you as submitting author. The synopsis that fails to captivate an editor is apt to be banished, as well, into the wilderness of non-publication, with or without a meal. Tell your synopsis story in the most compelling and riveting manner you can manage. Keep that editor leaning ever closer to the fire, all the way from "Once upon a time" to "happily ever after."

At the opposite pole from those authors who don't take the synopsis seriously enough are those who take it too seriously. One writer I worked with, Lisa, was a twice-published historical romance author known for her dense plots and complex characters. She was at the point in her career where she could sell her next novel on the basis of a proposal. Instead of writing the complete story up front, she could submit the first one hundred or so pages of text, plus a synopsis, to her editor and be considered for acquisition and publication. Unfortunately, Lisa insisted she could not write a synopsis. She slogged through the entire 120,000 words before making her submission. By that time, her editor had moved on to another publishing house, and her replacement was less than crazy about Lisa's work. I was Lisa's agent, and we did manage to get a contract eventually, but not under as generous terms as would have been probable with the previous editor.

Too many authors feel just as stymied as Lisa did. There's a rumor that synopsis writing is excruciating at best, impossible at worst. I contend that it doesn't have to be. If you can write a novel, you can certainly write a synopsis. Besides, you have no choice. As I said earlier, the synopsis is the accepted and expected form in which you will present your story. No editor is going to read your complete manuscript these days. They weren't willing to read Lisa's first manuscript in its full-length form either, even though they requested she submit the complete manuscript along with her synopsis. They just wanted to make certain she actually had a complete manuscript. That is the general editorial attitude toward unpublished authors. The editor wants to make certain you can actually go the distance of writing an entire novel. Nonetheless, that complete manuscript won't be enough—they will require a synopsis.

Don't let yourself be caught in Lisa's trap. Don't tell yourself you can't write a synopsis. Don't let your fears get the better of you. To counteract that fear, and to extricate you from the Lisa trap,

I've come up with something I call the painless synopsis technique. I will tell you how to use that technique in detail, but first some more about what a synopsis is and how it should be written.

Begin by getting off to the same fast start I recommended for your novel. You need a dramatic opening here at least as crucially as you did for the opening of your story. You need an opening line that has been crafted into a truly stunning narrative hook. Keep in mind that many editors and agents read the synopsis before they even look at the manuscript, just to make certain this is the type of story they're looking for. This means the first line of your synopsis will be the first line they read. Make it count to your advantage.

Then move directly into your story. Don't amble in. Start where the excitement of your story starts, when the blood is on the floor, and not a moment before. Never begin with backstory, the details of what happened to your characters, or the roots of your story situation. Never begin with description of characters, setting, or anything else. You can feed in these details later in the synopsis, gradually, never in large doses, and only as they are absolutely needed for the editor to understand the present action of the story as you are relating it.

Begin your synopsis in the same way you must begin your story as a whole: with conflict. Circumstances are already in motion. These circumstances plunge your protagonist, right here in the first paragraph of your synopsis, into the dilemma that is both the reason for this story being told and the story's focus of interest for the editor or agent you are trying to attract. The degree of intensity and drama in this opening will determine how deeply your narrative hook is set, how high the level of editor interest in your work will be.

Before writing further, think about your story. What are the main points? What are the complications that beset your protagonist, the obstacles that intervene between your protagonist and his goal in this story? Do your complications escalate in seriousness as your story progresses—what initiates these complications? How are they exacerbated? How are they resolved, or not resolved? What is the climactic scene of your story? How does your story end? You must work out these final elements—the climax scene and the ending—in a fair amount of detail in the synopsis. By doing this, you assure the editor that you have a satisfying and effective resolution for your story and that you know how to make that resolution work as a storyteller.

Write your synopsis in the present tense and in third person. Do not debate me about that, please; this is simply the way it is done, so do it. Make this your snappiest, most compelling writing. Be careful, however, that the tone of the synopsis is appropriate to the tone of the book you are writing. For example, don't write a chirpy, chatty synopsis for a dark suspense story. And as I've said before, begin with the first chapter of your story and proceed from there to the ending. If you are sending sample chapters, the action from those chapters also must be included in the synopsis.

Pay special attention to the verbs you use in your synopsis. Use the strongest, most precise verbs you can to communicate what is happening in your story. Write with a thesaurus at your side. Always favor strong verbs in the place of adjectives to maximize expressiveness. Use action verbs to create and sustain a sense of the intense and riveting action that is ongoing in the story you are showcasing. This is extremely important, as is use of the present tense to give that action an immediate feel.

Write your synopsis in the form of a running story summarized. Tell the story in chronological order. Never write it chapter-by-chapter with those chapter divisions identified in any way. The object is to immediately hook the editor into your story and keep him hooked via the suspense and relentlessness of your storytelling. Chapter demarcations, or any other device that might distract the editor from that unwinding story, are absolutely verboten.

For similar reasons, do not include separate sketches of your characters with your synopsis. Instead, insert a very brief description whenever a main character is introduced. Remember my previous discussion of the closely observed detail? Employ that principle here. Focus on the basic nature and personality of this character, rather than on her physical appearance. Do not include the character's age unless it is relevant to understanding the story. To capture the essence of this character in a phrase, nothing less than your sharpest, most insightful writing is required. Secondary characters need almost no character description in the synopsis, other than to identify briefly their function in the story. Use specific names for all characters and places. Otherwise, your story will feel vague, inadequately imagined.

Never submit what I call a to-be-continued synopsis. This is a grievous synopsis sin committed most often by authors of mystery and suspense. They think they will intrigue the editor or agent by leaving the story ending a mystery. In other words, they leave it out. Think again. This is yet another case of being too clever—or deceiving yourself into believing you're too clever—for your own good. Busy editors have no time for such shenanigans. That editor wants to know how your story ends. Depriving her of this knowledge is your ticket to the rejection pile.

Balance the synopsis in proportion to the book in terms of length. The first half of the synopsis should cover roughly the first half of the book. The second half of the synopsis should cover roughly the second half of the book. The exception to this rule of thumb is the ending. As I said before, you must work out the climactic scene and ending in some detail in your synopsis. For that reason, the segment of your synopsis recounting those events may be somewhat disproportionate in length.

I emphasize this admonition regarding proportionate length because too many authors disregard it. Half or more of their synopsis may be taken up with recounting only the opening chapters of the story. This is a particular offense of authors who are at the point in their writing careers where they can sell a book to an editor on the basis of only a proposal made up of opening chapters and a synopsis. Since the beginning of the story is all they have actually written, that beginning occupies the lion's share of the synopsis as a whole. This reflects an attitude of complacency, even overconfidence, on the part of the writer.

Every author should keep in mind that this is an insecure time in publishing, for published and unpublished alike. In fact, getting published and staying published, especially well published, has never been a walk in the park. This is a tough business to break into and a tougher business to stay on top of. No one can afford to submit anything less than her very best effort—and that includes the synopsis—to an editor or literary agent these, or any, days.

Do not act out or dramatize your story in the synopsis. This is telling your story as opposed to showing it, and is exactly the opposite of what you are supposed to do in writing the story itself. The one exception to this synopsis-writing rule is the occasional insertion of a line of dialogue. This must be a powerful line of dialogue that presents the drama of the story, at its present juncture, more forcefully than narrative ever could. Even so, quote only an occasional line, no more.

As you tell your story in synopsis form, stick to the story line. Do not wander off track. And do not overexplain. You are telling us the meat of your story. Don't get bogged down in the side dishes, the details that describe the main action of the story but are not that action itself. At the same time, it is imperative to avoid writing what will read like a catalog of events—this happened, then that happened, then another thing happened. How monotonous! Avoid monotony at all costs.

Make sure enough is happening in this story to fill a whole book. The editor is examining this synopsis to determine whether or not you have enough material, meaning story and character complexity, to sustain a compelling full-length manuscript. Nonetheless, you must not contrive incidents merely to occupy space and fill pages. Nor should you contrive events for the sole purpose of creating non-stop action. Each story event must arise from what happened before and must lead to what happens next, in a cause-and-effect continuum from beginning to end.

Avoid storytelling clichés. Use the process of writing your synopsis to detect such clichés in your story, and other problems as well. Correct these problems, in both the story and the synopsis, before submitting to editors or agents. Other story weaknesses to look for as you prepare your synopsis include outlandish plot developments, jumps in action without sufficient transition, and places where the pace of the story lags. Thus, the synopsis writing process becomes a significant step in the process of revising and polishing your story.

All of the above instruction may have you more stymied than ever about your ability to write a strong synopsis. I apologize for that, but you need to know and understand how crucial the quality of your synopsis is to how your submission will be received by an editor. Besides, you need have no fear. Any synopsis stress you may be feeling is about to be relieved.

THE PAINLESS SYNOPSIS EXERCISE

Phase One: A Tape Recorder, a Jug of Wine and Thou. Gather these materials in a cozy spot. Teetotalers, feel free to substitute mineral water or whatever. The "thou" should be any individual with whom you feel comfortable sharing your work, preferably someone who enjoys and appreciates the kind of story you write. Have a relaxing sip of refreshment, and turn on the tape recorder. Tell your story aloud to your one-person audience. Tell your story in whatever sequence it occurs to you. Be sure to include all the elements of that story—each of the characters, all of the scenes—from beginning to end.

Phase Two: Stacking the Deck. When you are alone, play back the tape. Using index cards, write a one-sentence description of each scene on a separate card, as you hear each scene being spoken of on the tape. Take as long as this requires, stopping the tape and replaying sections as needed. When you have finished, you should have a stack of approximately forty-five to sixty scene cards, depending on the length of your novel. Arrange these cards in order of story sequence.

Phase Three: Floor Play. Sit on the floor and spread the cards around you in the order they occur in the story. I prefer a sunburst arrangement myself. Look for gaps and bulges in the story line—places where there is too little action or too much—for pacing and clarity purposes alike. Add or subtract cards accordingly. If you don't yet know what specific scene you will add to your story to fill a specific gap, place an empty card in that position with a question mark on it. That way you will know you need to come up with a scene there, one that evolves from the story action and developments that precede it. Make sure your cards for the conclusion of your story are sufficient to convince the editor you have a story ending that will satisfy a reader. Gather the cards into a sequential pile.

Phase Four: Cutting the Cards and the Task Down to Size. On one card at a time, in story order, write two or three carefully crafted sentences that present that scene at its most intense, most moving, most conflict-ridden. Brainstorm any scenes you need to add to fill gaps in pace or understanding. Make sure these cards define the action of each scene in your strongest, most compelling writing.

Phase Five: Don't Forget the Players. Whenever a character is introduced into the story, at that point in your card pile and attached to that specific scene card, add another card with a description of that character in a tightly written phrase or sentence at the most. Craft that description with careful attention to the closely observed detail, as I have discussed earlier in this segment.

Phase Six: For Openers. On a separate card, write a superb opening sentence that is concise, straightforward, and startling—one that only an editor ready for the pallbearers will be able to ignore. Polish this sentence into a true gem to open your synopsis in truly sparkling fashion. Keep in mind that this sentence could do triple duty—as the opening sentence of your proposal, as the opening sentence of your cover letter to the editor or agent, perhaps even as the opening sentence of your novel.

Phase Seven: There You Have It. Type your synopsis directly from your card pile, turning over one card at a time and typing what you've written there. Throw in a transitional sentence or two, where needed, to make the telling run smoothly.

Phase Eight: The Winning Result. That result is twofold: a short story without dialogue or too much description, and a synopsis that could sell your book.

Secret #47: Pitch Perfect

A pitch is your story succinctly defined in a high-impact paragraph that is dramatic, compelling, and brief. High-impact is the key phrase here. The purpose of your pitch paragraph is to knock an editor's socks off. Imagine it is late in the evening. This editor is couch-deep in the stack of manuscript proposals she's brought home because she never has time to read them at the office. Her eyes are tired from reading too small fonts and too light print under artificial light. She can't help feeling at least a little resentful that she can't have an evening to herself, because the job she loves takes all day and into the night to accomplish. Worst of all, most of what she's read this evening, with few and fleeting exceptions, has been mediocre at best. Your manuscript proposal is next on her pile.

This may sound like a hopeless scenario for the submitting writer. However, in a way, this scenario can function to your advantage. What you have to do is figure out how to give the editor the thing she wants and needs most at this moment. I can tell you from personal experience that she wants and needs to be surprised. Nothing turns an editor on more than to recognize the flash of talent on a page.

The first page that any editor or literary agent will see is your cover letter. How do you create a flash of originality in a letter? Letter writing is not the most creative form of written communication, at least not when it involves the prosaic, informational, business-style single cover page for a manuscript submission. Nonetheless, you must burn through that humdrum form with a spark hot and bright enough to ignite an editor's overtaxed and dulled-out interest. How in the name of heaven do you accomplish that?

The answer I suggest is the pithy and perfect pitch. I further suggest that you "go Hollywood" to get it. The screenwriter pitch is a cliché in our culture. Still, the high concept prevails as the quickest, most pointed way to attract attention to a story idea. Hollywood writers and agents notoriously marry a couple of well-known movie titles to create a startling, or at least positive impression on a film producer or director. Endless jokes have been made about absurd combinations—*Godzilla* meets *Pretty Woman* and the like. You would be well advised to stop laughing and start learning.

Toy with a few combinations, unrelated to your story, to get the feel of the process without the pressure of the anxiety about presenting your own work. Say, for example, *The Terminator* meets my old favorite, *Gone with the Wind*. What kind of story would have that as its high concept? What kind of story would be pitched in those terms? How about a historical fantasy? What other possibilities can you come up with? Get yourself thinking of story essentials in these shorthand terms.

I understand how difficult it is to do this with your own story. You are too entwined with the complexities of your story and the interactions of your characters to imagine encapsulating all of that into a sentence or two. It feels like a trivialization, even an insult to your work. You might need help here, preferably the help of another writer with his own work ready to be pitched to editors and agents.

A brainstorm session with this other author is in order. To prepare for the session, write down the information your brainstorm partner will need. Following are the points you need to define for your partner as succinctly yet descriptively as you can:

- The main character/protagonist—with an insightful description, perhaps the one you worked out from the previous segment about synopsis writing
- The love interest—if that is a significant element in your story
- The antagonist—your protagonist's nemesis in this story
- The setting—the time and place your story happens
- The situation—conflict so intense between your protagonist and antagonist that your protagonist was compelled to act, and that you were compelled to write the story of what happened
- A motivation—whatever it is that compels your protagonist to act in this situation

This is the raw material you bring to your pitch brainstorming session. I prefer the single brainstorm partner arrangement to a group, because one-on-one interaction focuses energy and inspires intimacy. In my experience, this arrangement produces the most intense experience and the strongest results for my work. You decide what arrangement works best for you. Within that framework, there are, however, universal rules. Here they are for a two-person session. Adapt them, as you require, for your own session parameters.

- Designate the time limit of the session. I suggest a half hour, never more than forty minutes.
- Devote half of the session to one person's story, the other half to the other's. Decide which order you will go in up front.
- Determine a method of documenting responses. I prefer a tape recorder, because it allows both of you to be free to think and speak without the interruption of writing things down.
- Read your story points (the ones you developed earlier in this passage) aloud before beginning the half of the session devoted

to your story. Don't begin timing the session until that reading is finished and you have answered, briefly, any points of clarification your partner requires. Make sure this explanatory period is dispensed with as fast as possible. Save your mental energies for the actual brainstorming.

- Together—by brainstorming ideas, blurting out whatever comes to you, bouncing off each other's creativity, or using whatever method of exchange works for the two of you—craft one sentence describing the story being discussed. Then, if you'd like to go further, create a second sentence. Write absolutely no more than three. These should be short, punchy sentences. Remember that conflict is the essence of story.

- When the first half of the time limit has passed, take a moment to write those sentences down while they are still fresh in both of your minds.

- Continue, first reading the story points for the second person's project, then brainstorming that project the same way you did the first.

- Review each of the resulting pitch paragraphs. Answer the following question regarding your partner's pitch, and do your very best to be honest, though, of course, tactful: "Would you—as an editor or a reader—buy this book? If so, specifically what would compel you to do so? If not, why would you not be compelled to do so?" Then, have your brainstorming partner respond to the same questions regarding your manuscript. Record those responses.

- Work together to figure out how the responses to the above questions might be utilized to revise the pitch and make the two stories, as they are currently written, come across to an editor as more marketable.

- Later, when you are on your own, listen to the tape recording of the segment of the brainstorming session regarding your story. Reread the resulting pitch paragraph. Is this paragraph true to the story and characters you have created? Use any untapped ideas from the tape recording to deepen that truth and to intensify the impact of your pitch.

Include this pitch in the cover letter for your submission, as close to the opening of that letter as possible. I recommend that this pitch be the second paragraph of your cover letter, but that is far from the only place a strong pitch can be used. Copy or type it onto a card. Present this pitch card at writers conference editor and agent interviews, or in any other venue where you want to capture interest in your story. Use it after publication, as well, for promotional pieces and the like. Craft and polish this pitch into a single unforgettable sentence. The result will prove worth the effort many times in the career of this project. You can take my word on that.

Secret #48: Promote Yourself—Yes or No?

I still hear authors debate self-promotion long after the question has become moot, in my opinion. Should I promote myself? Should I not? This is really just a way of asking, should I spend the money and the effort, or should I not? The answer is clear as glass to me: Yes, you should. I have represented two authors of relatively similar writing talent. One promoted her work. The other did not. The author who did the self-promotion had measurably more career success than the other author did.

The commercial fiction business has a lot to do with numbers. When it comes to staying alive as an author—and by that I mean, continuing to be well and enthusiastically published by your publisher, or moving on to another publisher under favorable contract circumstances when that is the best option for your career—the commercial fiction business actually may be *all* about numbers. You always must be selling in numbers, greater numbers with each book published under your name. And numbers are all about name recognition—not just title recognition, but name recognition.

Way back in the 1980s, Stephen King wrote an essay called "On Becoming a Brand Name," which recounts his evolution from a total unknown to a household word. Stephen King certainly is a brand-name author. His name is better known than his titles, and that is what being a brand name is all about. Other authors have achieved similar status. Some may have contributed to that rise with their own promotional efforts. Some may not have. Stephen King did not. However, he is Stephen King, not only an author, but a phenomenon. The collection where his essay appears as the foreword, *Fear Itself: The Horror Fiction of Stephen King*, has a lot to say about why he is such a huge success in terms of numbers of books sold, filmed, etc. Most of us are likely not publishing phenomena, but we do want to make our names as well known as we can manage.

Name recognition is the key to success as a popular fiction novelist. First and foremost, of course, you must be a talented storyteller. No amount of hype, however skillfully executed and advantageously placed, can camouflage a dull story. The previous passages of this book are all about how to create an intense, dramatic, compelling yarn—the kind of story that is the real secret to Stephen King's success and to that of others like him. This passage, on the other hand, is about what to do *after* you have written the most intense, dramatic, compelling yarn you can.

First you have to recognize and accept an unpleasant reality, unpleasant because it probably isn't what you want to hear. That reality is this: Your publisher will make little or no effort to promote your work until your career as a selling novelist has taken on a momentum of its own. Before that happens, your publisher will not consider you worth the investment of time and resources that promoting your work and your name would require. This may not be what your publisher professes. In fact, your editor, backed by the company publicist, may promise to back your book to the hilt. Believe those promises at your own peril. Unless there is a clear-cut, obvious reason to anticipate strong sales of your book, with or without publicity, your publisher will commit zilch to promotion.

A former client of mine learned this lesson the hard way. The editor had seen my client lecture and was a fan. I believe this editor sincerely wanted to make my client's book a big success. This editor wooed my client, took her out for expensive lunches, and promised her the moon. I told my client to take those promises with a grain of salt. It was my job, as her literary agent, to let her know that the publicity efforts her editor described were not likely to happen, that my client should rely on her own marketing savvy and knowledge of her audience. She didn't listen.

Even when the print run numbers turned out to be considerably lower than we'd been led to expect, she kept faith in her editor's promises. Next, the publicist assigned to the book defined its potential audience much more narrowly than was good for my client's interests. That narrow definition limited any outreach the company might make on behalf of the book. Even then, my client latched onto her editor's justifications for that limitation and continued to believe them.

It wasn't until my client received the itinerary details for her brief publicity tour that her eyes were finally opened. Only two book signings had been set up in the first city on that tour, a city that should have been a major market for the book. The publicist's limited vision of the book limited the number of bookstores he thought would produce enough sales to be worth the effort of arranging a signing. Who knows? Maybe limitations on the publicist's time were a factor, as well as his awareness that the small print run meant the company wasn't a thousand percent behind this book.

Whatever the scenario on the publicist's end, my client had been hung out to dry. It was too late to make up for the squandered opportunity of this tour city. No media appearances had been planned. Additional bookstores would have been willing to host signings, but there was no time to make those arrangements now. My client got on the phone and personally invited everybody she knew in town to come to the two signings that had been scheduled. She encouraged them to bring friends and spread the word that she would be conducting workshops at both signings.

Because of those calls, and the word of mouth about my client's talent as a workshop leader, the turnout at the signings was good. Unfortunately, there weren't sufficient copies of the book on hand to accommodate the number of potential buyers. Apparently, the publicist's limited aspirations for the book were shared by the booksellers. Their orders had been modest. In the end, this strong sales venue was squandered, along with my client's heroic eleventh hour efforts, because of the less-than-heroic efforts of her publisher. She had learned a valuable lesson at an unfortunate cost.

I reiterate this incident at such length because it is crucial that you learn the same valuable lesson, but without the cost. I'm not suggesting that you challenge your editor's claims, or the publicist's. That will create defensiveness, even resentment, which won't help your career or your relationship with your publisher. I do suggest that you push for whatever you can get from them on behalf of your book. I also urge that, regardless of what they promise, you move full speed ahead with your own promotional campaign, prepared to take up the slack if your publisher's promises fall through.

I use the term campaign in a battleground sense because this is, in fact, a war to win the ground of audience attention for your book. You must become a warrior for this book and for all your books that will follow—a warrior on behalf of your career. Plan your battle strategy, in detail, several months ahead of the publication date for your book. Read up on publicity tactics. I recommend *Guerrilla Marketing for Writers: 100 Weapons to Help You Sell Your Work* by Jay Conrad Levinson, Rick Frishman, and Michael Larsen, and *1001 Ways to Market Your Books* by John Kremer.

I'm not in favor of letting your editor in on your book promotion plans before you implement them. My client did that and was told her plans could interfere with those of the publicist, the same publicist whose plans never materialized. My choice would be to keep a detailed record of everything you do, including times, dates, any documentation, and copies of any visuals you have used. After the book has been published and you have enacted all or most of your plans, organize this record into report form, and submit that report to your editor and your on-staff publicist. Keep a copy for your own reference, as well.

This is a tall order, I know. You may feel daunted by it and, perhaps, a little resentful. Shouldn't the publisher be responsible for attracting attention to his own product? Yes, in a more perfect world, the publisher should take that responsibility and initiative. But this is not a perfect world. This is reality. Don't waste energy grousing against the way things happen to be. Take this word to the wise and run with it. The plan's the thing. Get your planning started as soon as possible.

Secret #49: Promote Yourself—How To

I share with you a few pointers from my own experience, and that of my clients. For the most part, you can undertake these initiatives yourself, without professional assistance and on a limited budget. The titles mentioned above, by Levinson and Kremer, have more detailed advice and wider priorities to offer. I propose simply getting you started with the following commandment as your guide: Thou shalt promote thyself shamelessly. How do you do that? Add some basic principles to your own ingenuity.

Basic One: The Mailing List. One difference between a published author and a well-published author is a well-stocked Rolodex—in other words, an effective mailing list. The time to start collecting your own mailing list is yesterday. The first step is to acquire a business card of your own, if you've not done so already. I recommend a simple design with black, uncomplicated typeface on white card stock. Present only the basic information needed: name, mailing address, phone number(s), e-mail address, and Web site address, if you have one.

Once you have the card, give it away. Attend writer's and reader's events, and collect cards from everyone you can. These are warm contacts, people you have at least been in the same room with at one time or another. Cards collected at book-related events belong to people who are readers and who, therefore, might be interested in reading your work.

Hot contacts are those with a more personal relationship to you and a more personal awareness of your writing. These, of course, get priority in the Rolodex. Be sure to differentiate between hot, warm, and cool contacts. Cool contacts are people who you've never met, but have a connection with the book business or with the subject matter of your book. Think carefully before investing much in cool contacts, usually sourced from various organizational mailing lists. It won't hurt, however, to keep such lists. They may prove useful some day.

E-mail address lists are also useful. If you are going to promote your work via e-mail, use an effective graphic to do so, rather than a straight prose message. Learn how to send that message without a long list of destination addresses at the top. Such a list belies any illusion of private communication and diminishes impact by requiring that the reader scroll down before finding your message. Compose your message, and select the graphic to have such impact.

Basic Two: Review Coverage. Research and make a list of publications, non-print, media, and Web sites that review books, especially books in your genre or category. Do your homework. Keep adding to this list. If possible, find out the deadline for each publication and media resource, and how far in advance of publication time you need to submit a copy of your book for it to be eligible for review. Find out to whom on the staff, specifically and by name, your book should be submitted. Your book's publication date will determine which issue or bulletin might carry a review of your work.

Don't be discouraged if certain publications or media outlets ignore your book submission and fail to review your work. Don't give up. Send them your next book, and the next. Eventually, they are likely to give in and review your work. I share with you a second commandment: Thou shalt persist. If you keep publishing and keep your titles in front of these reviewers, they just might give in to your persistence.

Instead of sending a copy of the finished book, which requires you to wait until the book is published to obtain copies, create faux galleys. The real galley proofs your publisher puts out are too expensive to acquire. Make your own by setting up two reduced manuscript pages on legal-size paper. Copies of these fake galleys are inexpensive and handy to send out to potential reviewers.

Enclose a SASE (self-addressed stamped envelope) with each reviewer submission, requesting to receive a copy of the issue reviewing your book. Reviewers may or may not comply. Try to collect as many of the resulting reviews as you can, by whatever means you can. Composite your reviews by cutting them out and pasting them up on pages and making copies suitable for inclusion with your next manuscript submission, or for any other purpose that could further your career. Include only favorable reviews in your composite. Send copies of these pages to your editor and to anyone else potentially influential in advancing your career.

Basic Three: Media Coverage. This is somewhere between tough and impossible to get. Start where you have the most chance, in your local region. Put together a press kit. Mine includes a professional biography, an upbeat and sharply written Q and A about my history in writing and publishing, a list of my publications, a composite of my best reviews, and a glossy photograph. I include a separate press release for each mailing. I place that release on top of the rest with the photo in the facing pocket of a dual-pocket folder.

I write the release with a strong news hook and one-liner message points. Study the principles of publicity writing if you are going to prepare these and other media pieces for yourself. Coming up with a news angle—something that will make the media want to interview you in particular—*is essential.* There are books on how to go about this, including those I've already mentioned. You might consider hiring a professional publicist to help you prepare these materials, as I have done for this book. You should plan on spending at least some of your advance money on promotion.

While focusing on your local media, don't forget the smaller venues: neighborhood newspapers, local radio, even community bulletin boards. When you do book signings or make appearances, seek out these smaller venues, particularly the weekly newspapers, in that media market, as well. Don't underestimate these resources, where your material is more likely to find available column space than in larger publications. Talk radio shows can be very effective, especially if they are scheduled in drive time, the to-and-from workday hours. You will need a strong news hook to make it onto these shows, even in a small media market.

Basic Four: Book Signings. Avoid throwing a book signing to which nobody comes. Here's what you do to prevent that:

- Make an aggressive attempt at local media coverage: news hooks, local hooks, etc.
- Provide the host bookstore with flyers to distribute, starting two weeks prior to the signing.
- Send a personal invitation to everyone on your mailing lists for the bookstore area.
- Incorporate an entertaining or informative talk or workshop into each signing.
- Work with the bookseller to make your event a success. Signings cost stores money.
- Create an attractive setup of your book cover, a table cloth, giveaways, cookies, or candy.
- Offer to autograph left over copies of your book.
- Leave any flyers and promotional giveaways in the store.

I like something I call drive-by book signings. In my experience, booksellers like them, too. Locate several bookstores in a given area. Choose a day or a weekend for covering all of them. Notify the bookstore managers, by mail and a follow-up phone call, that you will be coming on that day to sign books. Stop at the store, introduce yourself to the store manager, sign all of your books that are in stock, and label each one with a sticker that says autographed copy. Have these stickers made up on your own and bring them with you. Make them eye-catching. Mine are DayGlo red. Leave flyers and giveaways at each store. Be sure to send a thank-you note to the managers of each store you visit. The expenses of such a mini-tour are tax-deductible.

Basic Five: Promotional Giveaways. These have been effective for me in the past. I advise avoiding bookmarks and cover cards, which I believe have been overdone. Come up with an item that suits your book's subject matter and is an attention-getter. Consider choosing this item in advance and writing it into your story somehow. There are wholesale catalog houses, like Oriental Trading Company, that sell such items in bulk at very reasonable prices.

Basic Six: Printed Pieces. Flyers, brochures, and newsletters are some of the printed pieces you might incorporate into your promotional campaign. Make sure flyers aren't too busy visually. Brochures can feature a strong excerpt from your book, favorable review quotes about your work in general, an image of your book cover, your photo, listings of your other publications, and your signing appearance schedule. Newsletters must be specifically relevant to this book. Keep the material upbeat and witty. Inside peeks at your writing process could work here, as long as they are entertaining. Include amusing anecdotes related to research or the book subject. Come up with a snappy news-letter title. My first one was called "Orr What? News." Be sure you have enough material to fill at least a three-column page, and that this material is as amusing as you mean it to be.

Basic Seven: General Mailings. Mailings are often the most expensive strategy an author undertakes. That's why so many resort to e-mailings. Note what I say about those above. I continue to believe that the most effective promotional piece is the one a potential reader receives in her mailbox and holds in her hand. Of course, that means your piece must not have the look or the feel of junk mail. It must be original in content and graphically pleasing. In other words, it must be memorable in a positive way. A personal letter can work once in a while. Time this mailing to arrive two to three weeks before your publication date. Be sure to include instructions for ordering the book.

Basic Eight: Paid Advertising. Funds for paid advertising must be planned for and spent with extreme care and in a very targeted fashion. The advertisement must reach as many potential readers as possible, realistically potential readers for your type of book in particular. Genre publications and fanzines can be very effective, especially if they happen to carry a positive review of your book in the same issue. The utility of paid advertising in anything other than this directly targeted manner is questionable at best.

Basic Nine: Online Promotion. This continues to be an evolving area, though sales do seem to be among the most successful functions of the Internet. Web sites with links to online bookstores, electronic magazines with review columns, and relevant bulletin boards and chat rooms can help visibility and name recognition. Unless you have considerable electronic and graphic expertise, I suggest hiring a professional to design your site and maintain it. A static site that never changes is a waste of your time and money. A potential reader will visit it once or twice and never return. I also suggest an interactive element, a way for the visitor to take part in your site somehow. Check out other author Web pages. Note what works best there. Adapt your own original approach. There are also lots of sources for researching this subject. Start studying.

Basic Ten: The Writers' Community. Writers are readers, as are the writers' groupies who hang around conferences and other such events. Place announcements about your book in writing organizations' newsletters. This is yet another mailing list you must put together. Again, a strong news hook will serve you well. The hook in this case can relate to your writing process in some attention-getting way. Consider including a short (no more than 750 words) but highly informative article for publication with your announcement and a schedule of your book signings.

Never underestimate the power of writers gatherings as a showcase for yourself, your name, and your books. Develop one to three workshop topics you might present at one of these gatherings. Present yourself to the event organizers long in advance, and suggest a topic or topics you might explore, preferably in your own individual workshop, or on a panel if that is the only appearance slot available. Bring along flyers, brochures, giveaways, books to sell, everything you have. Pass out a sign-in sheet to all workshop attendees. These are warm contacts for your mailing list, especially if your workshop is a success. Assure that success by favoring information over personal anecdotes in your presentation, with references to your book salted in.

Secret #50: Dos and Don'ts of Being a Pro

Some of what I say below I have said before in this book. I repeat those points here to emphasize their importance for you to behave as a professional writer and to be regarded as a professional, as well.

THE COVER LETTER

1. DO think of this as a business communication, not a personal one between you and the editor or agent. Keep the tone appropriate. Being chatty or off-hand makes an unprofessional impression when you must be in pursuit of the exact opposite.

2. DO use standard business stationery, preferably your own letterhead. No designs, colored paper, or cutesy touches. This is a strictly professional-to-professional letter, and professionals aren't cutesy.

3. DO address each submission to a specific editor who is an appropriate audience for your work. Editors change jobs frequently, so make sure you have the most current information before you submit.

4. DO make the first paragraph about your story. Begin with a punchy, original line to hook the editor's attention.

5. DO make the second paragraph about why this manuscript is appropriately submitted to this specific publisher. DON'T make general statements about how this is exactly what readers are looking for, that it is a potential best-seller, etc. Such statements lack verifiability and come across as unattractively boastful.

6. DO make the third paragraph about your history as a published author, if you have one. DON'T include non-professional credits such as work on the high school newspaper or your office newsletter. Only include self-publications if you can document their sales success. If this is your first novel and you are unpublished, simply say that. Note your study of writing and specifics of that study directly related to this book.

7. DO mention that you also have submitted the manuscript else-where, if that is the case. DON'T mention previous submissions that resulted in rejection of your work.

8. DO close simply: "Thank you for considering my manuscript. I look forward to your response."

9. DO sign the letter "Sincerely." DON'T use any fancy parting phrases. Type your name, followed by your address, phone num-bers, and e-mail address, unless this information is printed on your letterhead.

THE MANUSCRIPT

1. DO make your manuscript as perfect as possible—clean, with con-secutively numbered pages, free of inserts, printed in dark type, with one-inch margins all around.

2. DON'T allow cross-outs, typing mistakes, or dirty pages.

3. DO print your book title, name, and phone number at the top left-hand corner of every page, and the page number at the top right of every page.

4. DON'T send out-of-sequence chapters as sample text. Send the first chapters only.

5. DO include a title page. DON'T include a dedication or acknowl-edgments page.

6. DO start each chapter a third to halfway down the page with a capitalized heading.

7. DO repeat the title and author lines on the first page of the manuscript.

8. DO make a hard copy of the manuscript to keep in a safe place, along with a backup disk. Always consider the possibility that your submission could be lost or destroyed.

THE MAILING

1. DON'T truss up your submission package to look like you're send-
    ing it through a minefield. A padded—with bubble plastic, never
    gray fuzz—mailing envelope will suffice. Inside that envelope, place
    your proposal—the first three chapters and a synopsis—in a pocket
    folder secured by a rubber band, with your cover letter clipped to
    the folder cover. If you are submitting a complete manuscript—only
    in response to a specific request for that complete work—use a
    manuscript mailer box wrapped in plain brown paper. Both are avail-
    able at most office supply stores.

2. DO have the manuscript completed and polished before you submit
    your proposal, unless you have previously published full-length fiction.

3. DO enclose an SASE (self-addressed stamped envelope) for the edi-
    tor's response and a number-ten business-size envelope. DON'T ask
    for your manuscript to be returned or expect that it will be.

4. DO send your submission via regular mail unless otherwise specified
    by the editor or agent. Priority, express, or special delivery mail is a
    waste of your money, since it will almost certainly be weeks or even
    months before your submission is read regardless of what form of
    mail you use. Including a postcard for the editor to return acknowl-
    edging receipt of your manuscript is also questionably effective. Proof
    of delivery via the post office is more dependable.

5. DON'T call or e-mail the editor or publishing house to make cer-
    tain your manuscript has been received. This makes an unprofes-
    sional, overanxious impression.

AFTER SUBMISSION

1. DO write a polite inquiry letter or e-mail if you've had no response
    to your submission after a reasonable time, at least eight weeks.
    If four to six more weeks pass without a response, place a polite

phone call to the editor. Be calm, understanding, and professional, and expect that your manuscript has not yet been read. Ask when you can reasonably expect that reading to be done. If that suggested time period plus two weeks also passes without response, I suggest a polite e-mail saying you will be making further submissions to other publishers but would, of course, prefer to work with this editor and house above all others.

2.   DON'T agonize over a manuscript once it has been submitted. The best attitude toward your submission at this point is, "Out of sight, out of mind." DO achieve this attitude by beginning another novel immediately and becoming so engrossed in that story that you have no time or mental capacity for worrying about previous submissions.

TO KEEP IN MIND

1.   DO be realistic about the fate of unsolicited submissions to publishers. These manuscript packages often are dumped in a corner of the company mailroom or in a box or bin or on a shelf with scores of other such packages. At many publishing houses, they immediately are returned to the author or even discarded. These houses accept submissions from literary agents only. You need to determine if this is the case before submitting. At houses where unsolicited submissions are accepted, they will be read when there is editorial time left over from other duties, which isn't very often. Editors doing such reading are often at entry level in the company's hierarchy. This is the case no matter what editor you addressed your package to. Check the publisher's Web site and submit to an associate or assistant editor rather than a senior one. That way, you will be more likely to have your work read by your target editor. Agented manuscripts, on the other hand, go directly to the editor they've been sent to and are acted upon faster and taken more seriously than unagented work.

2. DO be aware that there is a buyer's market mentality among editors. They have more than enough manuscripts to choose from. They will acquire only the standout examples of both superior writing and storytelling. DO look carefully and objectively at your novel to make certain it is in that standout class. DON'T submit if it is not. DO be aware that literary agents have the same attitude and exacting standards.

3. DO be aware that most of what is submitted to publishers, especially unsolicited submissions, is mediocre, lacking the fire, vitality, and originality that constitute the kind of material editors are looking for. DO produce a manuscript so riveting, exciting, and intense that it will jolt the editor out of the malaise into which she has been lulled. DON'T submit unless you wholeheartedly believe your story is capable of doing that. DON'T abandon it either. DO write a stronger and more dramatic draft, or drafts.

4. DO realize that commercial publishing is a business and, like any business, should be researched and studied before you attempt entry. DO give yourself every opportunity to learn everything you can about writing and the publishing business. Join professional writers organizations, attend writers conferences, subscribe to writers publications, and read books about writing and publishing.

5. DO network with other writers whenever possible, sharing information and offering support.

6. DON'T be shy about promoting your name and your work whenever possible.

7. DO approach you craft and the business of writing as a serious professional endeavor on your part, never as merely a hobby.

8. DO think of yourself as a professional writer. DO insist that those around you treat you with equal seriousness.

9. DO welcome yourself to the ranks of the pros.

Crossroads

AN AUTHOR SELF-INTERROGATION

Here's another DO for you. DO give editors and readers what they want. Ask yourself the following questions to find out if your manuscript has wide reader appeal for a popular fiction audience:

- Does your story belong to an identifiable genre or category that already attracts a mass audience?
- Does your story feature an admirable character struggling toward a hopeful, reassuring end?
- Does your story pluck heartstrings, touch and move the reader, make the reader *feel*?
- Does your story include a conflicted romantic relationship?
- Does your story present adult sexuality in a manner appropriate to this situation?
- Does your story focus around a strong conflict situation?
- Does that conflict start immediately at the opening of the story?
- Does your story feature substantial characters, as opposed to flimsy ones?
- Does your protagonist have a lot at stake in this story?
- Does your story keep the reader asking, "What next?" in every scene and every chapter, preferably on every page?
- Does your story feature an intriguing background, a world or piece of the world most readers will find fascinating, perhaps even new and unfamiliar?
- Does your story entertain the reader?
- Does your story keep moving at a page-turning pace?
- Does your story have a triumphant ending?

Are You There Yet?

A HANDS-ON EXERCISE

THE GET-AN-AGENT EXERCISE

- Calm down. Check your agent-search anxieties at the door. You need all of your mental capacities engaged, common sense and good judgment in particular.

- Resolve to be a warrior on behalf of your career and to follow each of the following steps toward finding the strong representation you need and deserve.

- Accept the fact that, for literary agents, client selection is a business decision. Don't take agency rejections personally.

- Determine whether or not you need/want an agent by answering these questions:

   A. Do I need/want a business partner to handle the financial side of my career?

   B. Do I need/want an objective professional opinion of my work?

   C. Do I need/want a front person to advocate with publishers on behalf of my work?

   D. Do I need/want an advocate who knows the publishing business better than I do?

   E. Do I need/want an advocate to get me more money and a better contract deal?

   F. Do I need/want a professional confidant to advise me on the course of my career?

   G. Do I need/want an advocate on my side who knows and understands the inner workings of the publishing business better than any lawyer can?

- Begin your agent search by defining the kind of writing you do.

Go to the bookstore and find books similar to your own. Check the acknowledgments pages of each of these books for the name of the agent who represented that project. From these sources, compile a list of agents who handle the kind of books you write.

- Continue your search by speaking, in person or online, with published authors in your writing genre or category. Ask them about their experiences with agents. Use your common sense and good judgment to evaluate their comments. Add to your prospective agents list accordingly.

- Attend writers conferences and other events where agents appear in person. Watch how they behave, and listen to what they say. Employ your common sense and good judgment yet again. Add to your prospective list accordingly.

- Keep adding to this list as an ongoing exercise.

- Make a file of note cards with a section for each agent on your prospect list. Record on these cards everything you find out about each of your agent choices.

- Go to the Association of Authors' Representatives Web site at www.aar-online.com. Check your prospective agent list against the AAR members listings on the site. Note which of the agents on your list are members and which are not. Read about membership requirements. This will tell you why it is advantageous to be represented by an AAR member.

- Search the Web for each of these agents on your list. If they have Web sites, read what they have to say about themselves, noting any listings of published authors and titles they have represented. Record this information in your card file.

- Look up each of these agents and their agencies in *Literary Market Place*, *Writer's Market*, and any other agent resource references you can find. Record the information you find in your card file.

- Eliminate from your list, or relegate to the bottom, any agents who charge reading fees.
- Go through your card file and choose the six agents you would most like to represent you.
- Reread your manuscript and make a tough-minded decision about whether or not it is ready for submission to a literary agency that will be at least as discriminating in its judgments as an editor would be.
- If you determine that your work is ready for submission, prepare a professional submission package. Consult the Dos and Don'ts of the Being a Pro guidelines found earlier in this passage.
- Call the agency to check address particulars and find out who at this agency is presently accepting submissions. Realize that this may not be the specific person on your prospective agent list. Understand that, since they are colleagues, this more accessible agent could be a more realistic prospect for you.
- Simultaneously submit to the six agents on your final prospective agent list.
- Make follow-up contacts: at six weeks after submission, with a respectful letter; two to three weeks later, with a respectful phone call, pinpointing when you should call again; another respectful phone call after that time has passed.
- Expect not to be accepted for representation by any of those agents or agencies. Busy agencies with successful client lists are generally all but closed to new clients.
- With that in mind, submit your manuscript proposal to appropriate editors at appropriate publishing houses. Consult the Dos and Don'ts of the Being a Pro guidelines for preparing and following up on these submissions.
- Persist until you prevail—or until you have a stronger manuscript

and can repeat the editorial submission process. By "until you prevail," I mean, until you get a call from editor with a contract offer.

- Do not accept that offer, even verbally. Verbal contracts are legally binding. You don't want to be bound by anything just yet. Simply say you are thrilled, but you are in the process of negotiating for representation and you or your new agent will get back to this editor very soon. In the meantime, make sure you have written down everything this editor said.

- Get off the phone. Postpone your urge to hop up and down and cheer. Take out the list of your half-dozen preferred agent prospects. Prepare a script of what you will say when you telephone these agencies. Call each agent on your list, beginning with your number one choice and working downward. Tell whomever answers that you need to speak to (fill in the agent's name) because you have a contract offer from a publisher and would like said agent to negotiate the contract on your behalf. Therefore, you need to speak to this agent as soon as possible. Mention that you have submitted your work to this agent and reiterate the circumstances resulting from that submission.

- Understand that the level of agent enthusiasm in response to your telephone calls will depend on the relative status in the publishing world of the publishing house making you the offer. If this is a highly regarded publisher of serious standing, I predict you will find representation by the time you reach the last of your half dozen agents of preference. If the offering publisher is less than prestigious in stature in the commercial fiction marketplace, you may have to face continuing on your own, or via a literary attorney, for the duration of this particular project.

AFTERWORDS

A IS FOR ATTITUDE. D IS FOR DISCIPLINE. FORGET ABOUT B AND C.

A IS FOR ATTITUDE

Remember *The Little Engine That Could*? I'm full circle from talking about my grandma to being one, so sometimes I think in terms of children's stories these days. They teach the basic principles we adults would be wise to revisit on occasion. The little engine had one big line of dialogue: "I think I can." The engine was small. The task was large. Everybody said he couldn't do it. He did it anyway. The little engine had a positive attitude, and that made all the difference. Attitude is everything.

Your Attitude Toward Your Book: We've already talked about giving your book wide reader appeal, and you have to think in terms of doing that. Let's call those appealing story qualities the best-seller touch. You must think in terms of giving your story the best-seller touch. A story with the best-seller touch, boiled down to its essence, is a story with urgency, intensity, and drama that captures the reader's heart and soul and sells your manuscript to an editor. Keep your psyche on the side of that kind of story, and you'll have attitude on your side, as well.

Your Attitude Toward the Publishing Marketplace: On the other hand, creating a best-seller has nothing to do with chasing the market. Don't plug in elements to your story because they happen to be hot at the moment. Let's say that stories about rugged individuals climbing mountains and sometimes falling off them are the current rage, as they were for approximately a New York minute a while ago. That market condition doesn't mean you should write such a story, unless you happen to have a genuine writer's fascination for a character in that situation and what happens to him. Otherwise, you will create a passionless story without intensity, a story that is anything but involving and anything but genuine. Besides, think about the New York minute. The market you're chasing is most likely on its way out of vogue by the time you hear of it. Editors already have seen about as much of it as they can stand.

Your Attitude Toward Yourself: Confidence is crucial when it comes to success in the writing business or any other business. Confidence is neither arrogant nor self-important. Confidence comes from knowing, realistically, what you are good at. Then you simply keep expanding that area of competence, feeling deserved pride in yourself for each accomplishment. Confidence is doing scary things and taking risks, because that is how you reach beyond what is to what could be. Confidence is taking yourself seriously and making sure those around you do the same. Confidence is telling yourself you don't have time for writer's block and behaving as if that's true, because it is. Confidence is behaving as if you feel confident, even when you do not.

Your Attitude Toward Your Career: No doubt about it, you have to hustle. You have to decide how serious you are about being a writer, getting published, and staying published—and then you have to make those things happen. Times are tough in publishing, but when were times not tough in publishing? When times are tough, the tough get going. Trying to get published is like being a kid playing baseball and dreaming of the major leagues. In the publishing ballgame, the odds are stacked as high against you as they are against that kid. Realize that, accept it, and then get back to work. Be on constant alert for every career opportunity. When that opportunity comes along, recognize it, grasp it, and maximize it. Meanwhile, along the way, don't forget that success at anything means nothing if you fail as a human being. Just as a strong character is the key to storytelling, strong character is the key to success as a person. Character with a capitol C. So, maybe you'd better not forget about that letter of the alphabet after all.

Your Attitude Toward Editors: They are not the enemy. Do not be adversarial with them. Along with that confidence I talked about, develop some patience. Be understanding about the inevitable delays built into an editor's overcrowded work life. He will love you for it. Make him your ally by being his ally. Once he does have time to respond to your work, learn to be edited graciously. He'll respect you for it and love you even more. Remember that you and the editor are a team.

Your Attitude Toward Other Writers: Are you envious? Do you gossip? Do you go online to malign? Electronic chat is a godsend for cutting down on author isolation and for the fast exchange of information that can be useful, even crucial, as long as that information is accurate. Unfortunately, electronic chat also can be the information age conduit for negativity and maliciousness. Keep in mind that we are all on this bus together. Let's not spend so much time and energy trying to trip each other in the aisles.

Your Attitude Toward Writing: Have you forgotten the joy factor?

Has all of the other stuff—anxiety, envy, self-flagellation—obscured for you the reason you started writing stories in the first place? Wasn't that reason the love of doing it?

If you've forgotten the joy factor, then you truly do not have your psyche on your side, and an attitude adjustment is definitely in order. Somewhere along the line between your first yen to write something down and whatever level of obsession you may be at today, you said to yourself, "I want to be a storyteller." That continues to be your job—to tell the best story you possibly can, and to learn from that experience so you can write an even better story next time.

Telling stories has to be the primary source of your satisfaction. If you've gotten away from that focus, you need to rethink yourself, what you are doing, and how you are doing it. Most of all, you need to start *feeling* again. You need to get back to writing from the heart. Write with all of your compassion enveloping your character. Feel her feelings. Experience what she experiences. Be open and vulnerable. Lay yourself bare to the story. Let it happen to you and around you. One session of that kind of writing, and your positive attitude adjustment will be assured.

Attitudes That Trigger Failure: This can happen on many levels—let's get these out of the way fast:
1. Not having high enough standards
2. Playing at writing instead of taking it seriously
3. Thinking you don't have to study your craft continually
4. Not revising and polishing enough

Attitudes That Trigger Success: This also can happen on many levels. All of the clichés apply:
1. Let a smile be your umbrella.

2. Look for the silver lining.
3. Laugh and the world laughs with you.
4. You are what you eat. (How did that one get in there?)
5. Keep going deeper inside and trust what you find there.
6. Keep getting better and know you can do that.
7. Remember that writing is your dream, and keep on dreaming.

In a business where you often are not in charge anywhere near as much as you would like to be, attitude is one thing you can control, one thing you can change. Remember *The Little Engine That Could* and think you can. Then say a little prayer—because praying can apply here—that thinking it will make it so.

D IS FOR DISCIPLINE

The first and last step in your writing career, plus all of the steps in between, is about saying "Yes" to yourself.

"Yes, I am a writer."

"Yes, my writing matters to me."

"Yes, my writing matters so much to me I will carve out space for it in my life."

Carving out space in your life requires discipline. Discipline begins with writing every day. Of all the technique lectures, writing classes, and a thousand books like this one, nothing can take the place of developing this first discipline: the discipline of regular work.

I set the minimum limit of one page or one hour a day. Sit down in front of the typewriter, word processor, or blank page. Do one of the following: stay there, doing nothing else, for a minimum of one hour whether you write a word or not; or stay there until you've written a minimum of one page. You may, of course, write more than one page. Be sure to do so at your most creatively productive time of day.

I do not advise going on for hours and hours. After four hours of writing, much of what you produce will need to be corrected, deleted, or crossed out, depending on your writing medium. A session that long will likely burn you out for sitting down and doing it again the next day. That means every day, with two exceptions a year: one day off for your birthday, and one day off for a major holiday of your choice.

Do I sound like I'm joking? I'm not. Start that schedule today. Stick to it. A year from now, you will have written the full first draft of a novel, from start to finish, and maybe more, from a minimum output of one page a day. That is why you must develop this discipline before all others. Here are some additional reasons:

- To produce a body of work during the length of your career.
- To keep yourself too busy to become dispirited.
- To regard yourself as a serious, professional writer.
- To keep your head and heart inside your story where they belong.
- To program yourself to need a daily writing fix before withdrawal sets in.

Here are some additional disciplines you must undertake as well.

Discipline Your Work Environment: You may not be able to create a room of your own for your writing, but you need at least a corner of your own. A desk, a file cabinet, and some personal items will make this space yours, and keep it that way—just for you and your writing. Invest in sophisticated equipment that will produce a professional-looking manuscript—a good word processor, unless you are eccentric enough to object to computers. I recommend getting over that eccentricity if you intend to write commercial fiction with tight deadlines. Whatever your writing medium, never submit a manuscript with typos or mistakes. Invest in a spell-check program if your word processor does not have one. This is essential.

Discipline Your Commitments: Cut out everything you can. Take on nothing new. Don't volunteer. When approached, the appropriate response is, "Try me again next year." Feel free to repeat that response annually for as long as it takes to get your writing career not only off the ground but sailing aloft in the winds of success. Meanwhile, my only exception to the no volunteering rule is for activities that will advance your career and cement your professional connections. Even then, use your common sense and good judgment. Don't volunteer to coordinate a writers conference. Do volunteer to recruit editors and literary agents to attend that conference. Recognition of your name is essential on that side of the desk, as well.

Discipline Telephone Time: If you don't have an answering machine, get one immediately. Make two message tapes—a regular one and a workday one. The regular tape says whatever you like. The workday tape is to be inserted at the beginning of your daily writing period and left engaged until that period is finished. This tape announces that you are working, but will be taking and returning calls during hours you designate. My favorites are three to five in the afternoon. Turn down the volume so you can't hear the incoming messages as they are left on the machine. Turn off the ringer, as well, and put the phone in another room. Turn off your cell phone. Check messages at the end of your work period, and not before. If this results in missing a message that involves actual threat to life or limb, you may reconsider the practice. People will pout and complain for a while. Explain patiently how important this uninterrupted time is to you. If they truly care about you, and are therefore truly worthy of your concern, they will come to understand.

Discipline Your Online Time: The energy you potentially waste on the telephone may be a shadow of what you fritter away on e-mail, chat venues, and just plain surfing the Internet. Take a tight grip on this time right now. Define for yourself the specific hours of the day or evening you will go online. Stick to those limits. Avoid scheduling online or telephone time during the hours of the day when you are most mentally and creatively productive. Again, if chat buddies and e-mail pals object, explain patiently how important your writing time is to you.

Discipline Your Family: You will only be taken as seriously as you take yourself, especially by those closest to you. Instead of just saying you have writing to do, insist that you have to write and must not be interrupted. Keep insisting on that until the notion takes hold. As with the phone and computer, set specific hours. Post them on the refrigerator or the door of your work area or both. Again, there will be pouting and complaints, perhaps more than from your telephone and online friends. Again, explain patiently, as many times as is necessary. Eventually, you will prevail. Don't give up. This is a critical discipline area. Your ability to pursue your career depends on it. Delegate responsibility. As I mentioned at the start of this book, ask yourself, "Do I have to do this? Is there someone else who could do it well enough? Does it have to be done at all?" This interrogation is particularly applicable to domestic duties. Ask yourself, "Do I want to be known for my sparkling clean windows (substitute any household accomplishment here, from trays of cookies to perfect laundry) or for a shelf of books with my name on every spine?" Those are the choices at stake. Make them well.

FORGET ABOUT B AND C—BUT NOT REALLY

I've already covered C, the character issue. The letter B, simply stated, is for being strong. I'm referring to psychological strength, the kind of strength you've given your admirable protagonist. You need to be that kind of protagonist in the story of your own career—independent, intelligent, and determined—what we, as real-life human beings, strive to be.

What does it take to succeed as a writer? First, it takes a certain facility with words. I also hope you have a love of those words, and a love of language in general. Talent as a storyteller is required, though much of that can be learned from books like this one and teachers like me. Imagination is a gift. Some have more than others, but this facility can be nurtured and developed. I suggest ways of doing that earlier in this book, as well.

Persistence is crucial to succeeding, both as a storyteller and as an author in the publishing world. As I've said before, you must persist until you prevail. First and most importantly, persist in challenging yourself to be the best writer you are capable of being. Then, challenge yourself to be better than that, then better still, for as long as your writing days continue. Persist in your struggle to be published. All of this takes considerable psychological strength. Remember also that writing for publication is a field of endeavor where acceptance is the exception and rejection is the rule. This may take the greatest psychological strength of all. Everybody isn't going to like your work, especially not every editor and literary agent. I've said this before, but it definitely bears repeating: You must learn not to take rejection personally.

I know from my own experience how much strength is required for that. I've fallen short enough times to make the lesson clear. Maintaining a realistic perspective helps. Writing is what we do, not who we are. We are much more than that. When you come to understand and believe that truth, your survival in this business, still emotionally intact, will be nearly assured.

Rejection by an editor says one of two things: you have sent your manuscript to the wrong publisher; or that publisher has no need of this type of story right now. The publisher could be about to publish something too similar or could have recently done so. It could have changed the parameters of its list since you researched it, or could be about to make such a change. There are many reasons, all beyond your control, why your work might not be a good fit with any given publisher at any given time.

Or maybe your work was not yet ready to be submitted. Maybe the storytelling was not sufficiently strong and original. Maybe the writing style was not yet sophisticated enough to attract an editor. Maybe you were not yet adequately accomplished as a writer to be submitting for publication. Determining the reason for a given manuscript rejection requires a great deal of strength—maybe even too much strength to be asked of anyone. Nonetheless, you must develop such strength if you are to have any hope of success.

There will be times when you find this strength in short supply. That is when you can use a little help from your friends, your writer friends in particular. Forge those alliances now, if you have not done so already. Remember that this generosity must be mutual. Keep watch for those days when your writing allies are in need of support themselves. Offer that support with an open heart. Together, your odds of

survival in this business, and in life, dramatically improve. Y
find the struggle easier to bear, and more enjoyable, as well

Which brings me, at last, to my personal mantra. I
when all of this gets to be too much, as it inevitably will
voices of self-doubt, along with those of all the perso
you've ever known in your life, thunder in your ears t
not, after all, have what it takes. When you are certa
never hear the "Yes" you've been working and waiting
you cannot, for one minute more, do any of what thi
you to do. Remember my mantra, the mantra I share
my very last words, at least for now:

DO IT ANYWAY!

INDEX